WEAVING WISDOM

Sermons by
Mennonite Women

Editor, Dorothy Yoder Nyce

This book has been a project supported by WOMENSAGE,
a Resource Center for Mennonite Women, which began a
year ago in the Elkhart/Goshen, Indiana area. An
important goal of the Center is to "...build up a
network of women already in leadership or who are
evaluating their particular function in relationship
to the church. These women value being in touch with
each other to address theological ideas and spiritual
needs." Retreats and workshops are planned locally.
A newsletter explores issues of theology, and a grant
has been received to develop and make available several
workshops for interested congregations. Another project
receiving support similar to this sermon collection is
a Mennonite Women's Calendar, a rich resource about
our heritage.

Requests for additional copies of this book or for
permission to make multiple copies of any material
herein should be made to:

Dorothy Yoder Nyce
1603 So. 15 th St.
Goshen, IN   46526

ACKNOWLEDGEMENTS

The editor wishes to express appreciation for the following help or materials that contribute to this collection of sermons.

Thanks: - to the women and men who have consistently believed in and encouraged women who wish to be faithful to their gifts for preaching and teaching.
- to Bowers Printing Service of Iowa City, Iowa. Mary Lou has responded to questions, and with sensitivity to the project, met our printing needs.
- to Suelyn Lee for her striking graphics and knowledge of details related to design. She recently was graduated from Goshen College with an art major and will do free lance work this summer.
- to John, Lynda, and Gretchen Nyce for accommodating another book project--for knowing when to not interfere and when to pitch in, with ideas or to maintain our family living.
- to a special woman who made funds available for the initial cost outlay.
- to Nancy Lapp, Gayle Gerber Koontz, Ann Weber and Laurie Oswald for their expressive division page litanies.
- to Sandy Wiens, coordinator of WOMENSAGE, for support, of both the general and particular sort.
- to University Printing Service, Iowa City, Iowa for binding work.

Credits:
graphics - Several are from Moss Lotus, a book of Julia Spicher's poetry, (Pinch Penny Press/Goshen College), 1983. Used by permission.
- The Story division page graphic first appeared, with an Isa. text, on the 1983 Goshen College commencement materials.

printed
materials- "Parable of the Little Lump of Clay, by Arland Esch, appearing on p. 31 is from WITH, July/Aug. 1980, v. 13, no. 7, pp. 22-3. Copyrighted by Herald (Scottdale, Pa.) and Faith and Life Press (Newton, Ks). Used by permission.
- Free verse quoted on p. 11, from Henri Nouwen's book With Open Hands, copyrighted by Ave Maria Pr./Notre Dame, Indiana. Used by permission.
- Biblical texts appear in many sermons, too numerous to credit each one. More extensive quotes we wish to acknowledge include: REVISED STANDARD VERSION - Gen. 1 material (with some creative adaptations in P. Kauffman sermon; most Isa. texts scattered in different sermons; Luke 4:14-21. JERUSALEM BIBLE - Daniel materials cited in the D.N. Friesen sermon. AMERICAN REVISED STANDARD - texts cited by G. Roten. GOOD NEWS BIBLE - cited D.A. Friesen.

Contents

Preface

This book records the concerted birth of North American Mennonite women in the task of preaching. Admittedly, a few individuals have preached on occasion throughout our 450 year history. And our Dutch sisters have had considerable experience as preachers/pastors since 1911, the year when the first Mennonite women were ordained--Ann J. Allebach in Pennsylvania and Annie Zernike in the Netherlands.

During the past decade there has been cautious progress in offering space to Mennonite women within preaching ministry, in General Conference and Mennonite Church congregations. Resistance to the idea also prevails in places. Compared to the more than 600 Episcopalian women ordained since 1976, we Mennonites have only a few. Many who preach among us pursue vocations other than pastoral ministry. Since congregations, rather than bishops, determine policy, we Mennonites will understand and practice women's pastoral leadership differently.

Most congregations free to include women ministers have come to fully endorse them. Such positive experience will "go a long way" toward providing personal support to woman who themselves lacked nurture and modeling through women pastors. This collection comes, then, as further encouragement--women who feel isolated in the task will do well to hear what their sisters are saying. Not for the purpose of plagarizing from the pulpit, of course, but in order to claim the common task of proclaiming life and hope through the gospel message.

Sermons and preaching have intrigued, or been important to, me for a long time. I was definitely influenced by the diet of sermons heard throughout my teen and college years, plus the past twenty. John Y. Swartzendruber, Dick Allison, John H. Mosemann, and Peter Gomes continue to connect my church experience--both corporate worship and accountable actions --even though their diversity makes me laugh.

Further, I have a budding interest in nineteenth century sermons. My research among Protestant women has been rich. It focuses on these: Lucretia Mott (preacher for 59 years among the quakers); Anna Howard Shaw (the "greatest woman speaker"); Olympia Brown (48 years of preaching among the Universalists); Maggie Newton van Cott (Methodist evangelist who preached 339 times in 1871, whose efforts led to 75,000 conversions); Antoinette Brown Blackwell (the first woman ordained in the U.S., in 1853).

Perspective on religious thought can be gained from reading their sermons. Presumably, next century's historians will be able to partially assess our present Mennonite scene by using sources such as Weaving Wisdom.

Exposure to such a collection will assist all of us to internalize that women are preaching. We will more likely then change references to ministers; we will avoid using only the pronouns he/him/his. We will become more aware of the injustice fostered when consideration is limited to men for leadership that includes regular preaching. We who claim to be biblically faithful will give more attention to the first century

PREFACE

church's inclusion of women in all tasks. And our children will be able
to experience both women and men as convinced preachers and teachers.

To prepare and present sermons is an awesome task. Among other
things, it calls for disciplined study, sensitivity to the experience of
church members, honest respect for the biblical heritage, knowledge of
church history, time, and focused reflection. These are the components
to weave; beyond them comes wisdom.

Personal interest in gathering such a collection has been mine for
some years. I currently do not prepare sermons for a congregation on a
weekly basis, so I value volunteering time to get the word, from our sisters, to a broader audience. Fortunate are those who hear some of these
women regularly. And fortunate are all of us to have this "cloud of witnesses." "May their tribe increase."

Writers expressed genuine enthusiasm for this collection. Some also
expressed hesitations. One called herself a "total rookie." A black
friend assured me that most of her preaching is extemporaneous. Several
simply were "so drawn to experiences of congregation members" they could
not take time to choose from among several sermons. Another observed:
"Perhaps one is never really finished revising a sermon." Editing has
been done. But with care to preserve and value the fact that sermons
"speak." Delivery is crucial, for a listening audience. Hopefully, these
manuscripts retain the hearing quality.

Styles vary. So do preachers. Of interest are recurring threads--
the inclusion of hymns, references to birth and death, giving attention to
children, identifying with stories of biblical women, creating images,
using Isaiah content, being pastoral, and being personally vulnerable.
Sermons were only one component of the worship services; several authors
noted the importance of other people who were involved. Your reading
will be enriched if you also read scripture texts which are identified
but not printed here.

Weaving Wisdom is a statement about who we are--as Mennonites, as
women, as preachers/teachers. We have vigorous concerns and beliefs--
about spirituality, justice, and telling stories. Sermons express our
theology, our spirituality or way of attending to the fact that we are
religious, our care for our present world, our attempt to "find new ways
to communicate the old, old story." These offer good devotional material,
or they can be read with a friend or group to stimulate discussion. They
are a gift to all who will read them.

May wisdom be yours.

Dorothy Yoder Nyce
Goshen, Indiana
June 1983

Spirituality

A LITANY OF LIFE
Written by Nancy S. Lapp

Leader: Great God, Maker of us all,
          we acknowledge that our souls are shaped for Your Spirit.
          We bring to you all that would alienate us from Your Presence.
          Have mercy on us.

People: We come with our fear of rejection and failure
                  with our mistrust of others and ourselves
                  with our hurt and unwillingness to forgive
                  with our confusion and uncertainty
                  with our anger and frustration
                  with our pride and self-sufficiency.

All: Have mercy on us.
          Heal us and grow us into wholeness.

Leader: We listen for your Word.
          Speak to us in the deep places of our hearts.
          (Pause in silence.)

Leader: Thank you for making us in your likeness.

People: With creative ability
             with the capacity to give and receive Love
                with the power to communicate
                   with strength to forgive.

Leader: Teach us how to live Love.

People: Keep us on tiptoe with expectancy and Hope.
          Grant us Faith to risk new experiences.
          Give us Courage to develop and use the Gifts you've given us.

Leader: Thank you for the Word made flesh.

People: Incarnate in us the Word
          that you may be revealed in us.

All: In the name of Yahweh,
          the God who Creates, Redeems and Sustains us. Amen.

NANCY wrote this litany specifically for this collection. She and others
will no doubt use it in contexts of worship in the future.

Pilgrimage through the Wilderness
Anna Kreider Juhnke

Two weeks ago we celebrated Easter. That day Jewish people all over
the world were in the middle of the eight days of their Passover celebration. On the same night that we gathered around tables for our Maundy
Thursday communion service, Jewish families were gathering around their
tables for the Passover Seder meal. That's not a mere coincidence either,
because Jesus' Last Supper with his disciples was a Passover meal.

Passover celebrates the Exodus. The Exodus is the central event in
the Jewish faith. The core of it is the deliverance of the Israelites
from slavery in Egypt--the miraculous crossing of the Red Sea. But in a
broader sense, the Exodus is a whole series of events. Throughout the ages
the Jewish psalm writers and prophets praised God for the whole series.
Look, for example, at the list in Psalm 136:

God smote the firstborn of Egypt,
led the Israelites through the Red Sea,
led them through the wilderness,
and helped them conquer the land of the Canaanite kings to be their
own land.

Add one more event: the covenant at Mount Sinai. Between the Red
Sea crossing and the journey of forty years in the wilderness, Moses
brought the Israelites to Mount Sinai to learn God's law, the way God's
chosen people were to build their new society of justice and righteousness.

The Exodus, the covenant, the wilderness, and the Promised land--
that's the way God saved the Israelites and created them as a people. It's
the central event of Jewish history. But it is not the central event of
Christian history. Our central event is the crucifixion and resurrection
of Jesus. That's how God saved us and made us a people.

However, with a little imagination, Christians of the Middle Ages saw
how you wouldn't really have to choose between these two great events of
salvation. They saw the Exodus as foreshadowing the death and resurrection

3

of Jesus. A very old Easter hymn written before 750 A.D. just folds the Exodus right in (# 178, The Mennonite Hymnal):

> Come, ye faithful, raise the strain
> Of triumphant gladness;
> God hath brought His Israel
> Into joy from sadness;
> Loosed from Pharaoh's bitter yoke
> Jacob's sons and daughters'
> Led them with unmoistened foot
> Through the Red Sea waters.

The rest of the verses are explicitly about Jesus' resurrection. Another Easter hymn by the same poet, John of Damascus, again uses the parallel of the Exodus and the resurrection as saving events (# 174):

> The day of resurrection!
> Earth, tell it out abroad;
> The passover of gladness,
> The passover of God.
> From death to life eternal,
> From this world to the sky,
> Our Christ hath brought us over
> With hymns of victory.

Jesus Christ is our Moses leading us out of slavery and into eternal life.

That's a glorious vision. But I didn't find much of it as I looked through modern hymnbooks. We generally take hold of the Exodus events at a different place and make them much more individual. Yes, Jesus set me free from bondage to Satan, but we don't usually think of Satan as Pharaoh or of baptism as crossing the Red Sea, the way medieval Christians did. Our imagination picks up the Exodus events during the forty years in the wilderness while each one of us is journeying to our Promised Land, our heavenly home just beyond the Jordan River of death.

You can think of a lot of songs describing this journey. Many of them picture the pilgrim as all alone in the wilderness: "I'm just a poor wayfaring stranger/ A-traveling through this world of woe." I am tired, hungry, and thirsty. I tend to get lost. I pray urgently for God to help and guide me, remembering the manna that God gave the Israelites. Or the water that Moses struck from the rock. Or, remembering the guiding pillar of fire: "Lead, kindly Light, amid th'encircling gloom,/ Lead Thou me on;/ The night is dark, and I am far from home;/ Lead Thou me on."

This somber tone echoes in another favorite hymn, "Guide Me, O Thou Great Jehovah." Look at this hymn (# 311) with me. The first line sets the scene. I am a "pilgrim through this barren land." I am hungry, so I pray for manna: "Bread of heaven, feed me now and evermore." I am thirsty, so I pray for the water that Moses struck from the rock: "Open now the crystal fountain/ Whence the healing streams do flow."

The words make sense and give hope if you know the Exodus story of salvation. But if we know the secret key, the New Testament story of salvation is hidden here too for our hope and encouragement. We need the Gospel of John as the key. According to John 6:51, Jesus said, "I am the

4

living bread that came down from heaven; if any one eats of this bread, he will live forever."

Jesus also is the water of life, the living water. Remember that in John's Gospel, Jesus promised the living water that we would drink and never thirst again (John 4:14-15).

One more reference in the book of John is a little harder to recognize. John also sees Jesus as the pillar of fire that guides in the wilderness. Jesus said, "I am the light of the world. He that follows me will not walk in darkness but have the light of life" (John 8:12).

Well, by the time we find Jesus everywhere in the wilderness, we gain a different view of being a "pilgrim through this barren land." The land doesn't look so barren anymore.

And I'm not just alone with Jesus on this pilgrimage either. Other Christians are on this pilgrimage with me. We're marching to the Promised Land together, and that old gospel song, "We're Marching to Zion," is so joyful partly because of the fellowship.

Who else, besides friends and other church members, is with us on this journey? The book of Hebrews tells us that all of those Israelites in the Old Testament surround us on our way, as a cloud of witnesses. Hebrews 11 is the great roll call of heroes and heroines we read for our scripture this morning. Abraham and Sarah, Moses, Gideon, David, and even Rahab the harlot set forth on their journey of faith, as do we. As verse 10 says, "they were seeking that city that has foundations, whose builder and maker is God." Verse 13 says they knew they were strangers and exiles on the earth, and they never received what was promised, since God had foreseen something better for us. Verse 40 says that apart from us, they would not be made perfect.

Now here we are on our pilgrimage, says the author of Hebrews. We're surrounded by this great cloud of witnesses to inspire us. And chapter 12 goes on to speak of our goal. It says you have not come to Mount Sinai and its terrifying fire and divine voice. Instead (verse 22) "you have come to Mount Zion and to the city of the living God, the heavenly Jerusalem, and to innumerable angels in festal gathering,...and to Jesus, the mediator" of the gracious new covenant.

Rejoice, therefore! We're marching to Zion, the beautiful city of God, and all the heroes and heroines of the faith are marching with us to receive the promised kingdom!

We have already seen several Christian layers over the Exodus story. It's like the series of transparencies of the human body that you have seen in health classes. First the vital organs, and then overlay the blood vessels, and the nerves and bones and muscles one layer at a time to give the total vision.

I have one more overlay on the Exodus story to give the vastness of the Biblical vision of salvation. The last one is from the book of Isaiah.

The Israelites had suffered a disaster when they were taken into captivity in Babylon. They had lost their Promised Land--for what more was there to hope? But a prophet Isaiah arose in Babylon, and his message starts in Isaiah 40: "Comfort, comfort my people." He had a new vision of hope. There would be a new Exodus much greater than the first Exodus. The exiles would come streaming back across the desert from Babylon to their home on Mount Zion.

But this time everything would be transformed as they went. I will read from Isaiah 43, starting with verse 14. Notice how God reminds the Israelites of the path through the Red Sea in the first Exodus. And yet God promises to do a new thing, much better, when leading them out of this captivity:

> Thus says the Lord, your Redeemer,
>   the Holy One of Israel:
> "For your sake I will send to Babylon
>   and break down all the bars,
>   and the shouting of the Chaldeans
>   will be turned to lamentations....
> Thus says the Lord, who makes a way in the sea,
>   a path in the mighty waters,
> who brings forth chariot and horse,
>   army and warrior;
> they lie down, they cannot rise,
>   they are extinguished, quenched like a wick:
> "Remember not the former things,
>   nor consider the things of old.
> Behold, I am doing a new thing;
>   now it springs forth, do you not perceive it?
> I will make a way in the wilderness
>   and rivers in the desert."

The pilgrimage this time won't be wandering forty years in the desert. When the Lord says "I will make a way in the wilderness," that means a royal highway--"every valley shall be exalted and every mountain and hill made low. . .and the rough places a plain." (Isa. 40:4)

When the Lord says rivers in the desert, that doesn't mean just e-nough to drink on the journey; it means enough to turn the wilderness into a new garden of Eden, as in Isaiah 35:

> The wilderness and the dry land shall be glad,
>   the desert shall rejoice and blossom;
> like the crocus it shall blossom abundantly. . .
> For waters shall break forth in the wilderness,
>   and streams in the desert;
> the burning sand shall become a pool,
>   and the thirsty ground springs of water;

As the people journey on the highway, "the eyes of the blind shall be opened, and the ears of the deaf unstopped; the lame man shall leap like a hart, and the tongue of the dumb shall sing for joy." Everything and every-one is transformed. "And the ransomed of the Lord shall return, and come to Zion with singing, with everlasting joy on their heads."

This means more than a little band of Jewish exiles going back to re-build Jerusalem in 538 B.C. This is the Messianic age, the end times, the approach to the holy city of God, that new Jerusalem of eternal joy with which the Book of Revelation ends.

Isaiah sees this new Exodus as involving the whole world, not just the Jews. As he says in chapter 51:
The Lord will comfort Zion;
he will comfort all her waste places,
and will make her wilderness like Eden,
her desert like the garden of the Lord;
joy and gladness will be found in her. . .
for a law will go forth from me,
and my justice for a light to the peoples.
My deliverance draws near speedily,
my salvation has gone forth,
and my arms will rule the peoples;
the coastlands wait for me,
and for my arm they hope. (Isa. 51:3-6)

What a vision of the whole world redeemed! We can't see the holy city of God's new kingdom yet in our world of violence and injustice. We can't see the desert blossoming in the midst of pollution and strip mining. But we don't sit back in despair waiting for nuclear destruction. We work with hope for the renewing of our world. Because, to the eyes of faith, Christ has already started to transform this world. He has begun with us, with the Christian community.

And as we march to Zion, surrounded by the great cloud of witnesses from Jewish and Christian history, we can already see the flowers and rivers starting to spring up in the desert around us.

On our pilgrimage we pray, "Thy kingdom come; thy will be done on earth as it is in heaven." And we are granted a vision of the new Jerusalem, Zion, glorious city of our God, coming to earth, as John saw it at the end of the Book of Revelation. Thus, seeing God's pattern of salvation for the past, the present, and the future keeps the church moving forward in hope on its pilgrimage through the wilderness.

ANNA KREIDER JUHNKE preached this sermon at Bethel College Mennonite Church, North Newton, KS, April 25, 1982. She is an English professor at Bethel College. She serves on the General Board of the General Conference Mennonite Church and as Vice Chair of Mennonite Central Committee U.S.

Hope Revealed
Martha Smith Good

It was the sixth hour. My water pots, which had stood empty for a-
while, needed to be filled. This was my time to go to the well. You see,
everyone else went either earlier or later. I, however, did not dare to
go to the well with the neighboring women. I was an outcast. I was un-
acceptable. I was like garbage.

Even at this hour, I hesitated. The usual anxiety I experienced began
to mount as I forced myself to step outside. I was taunted, as usual, by
the neighboring children who shouted harsh, unkind words. "Sinner, bad
woman," they yelled, while their mothers made no attempt to silence them.
As each word echoed, it went through me like a sharp, hot, searing pain.
I was filled with anguish. Why was everyone so cruel? Why could I not be
accepted for who I was? Sure, I had broken a few rules, but was my offense
really unforgiveable?

As I neared the well, feeling the seeming hopelessness of my life, I
noticed someone perched at the place where I needed to draw water. Would
I go on? Could I go on? Who was waiting for me this time to hand out
condemnations? With pounding heart and trembling knees, I slowly went on.
Before I realized what was happening, the man spoke to me. "Give me a
drink" he said in a loving, gentle voice. I had rarely been addressed so
kindly. My first thought was to run! My mind was awhirl with confusion.

He was a Jew. I was a Samaritan. He a man and I a woman. In spite
of my fear, I stayed and we continued to talk. With my curiosity whetted,
I thought, Who is this man? He spoke as a prophet. This man was not condemning me--I was accepted. This man was challenging me--I was credited
as intelligent. This man was revealing his mission--I was trusted.
Gradually, hopelessness shifted toward hope. From this encounter, life
would have new meaning for me. Hooe was revealed. Life was restored.

John's story of the Samaritan woman points us to the encouraging news
that hope can be found in the midst of hopelessness. Perhaps that is

inevitable. Perhaps we can best experience the revelation of hope when life seems to be in despair. In a moment of desperate need we hope for anything better than the current pain. I recall a period of depression in my own life when each little word of encouragement or demonstration of love restored fresh glimmers of hope that life could go on. I could experience hope because, being in need of it, I was open to receive it.

As we reflect on the historical event of Jesus, we note that God was revealed through Jesus Christ at a time when the known world was most in need of a radical change. The people longed for new life--politically, economically, and spiritually. Those whose physical or spiritual need left them open and vulnerable were also the ones most ready to accept God's love and hope as revealed in Jesus Christ. Jesus sensed who was ready for him, who would accept the hope he could reveal. Although his coming was for all people, Jesus spent little time with those who believed they were spiritually secure and satisfied.

The faith, hope, and love which Jesus continues to offer can best be experienced by those who recognize their need for gifts and their access to them. I believe that we often miss out on God's spiritual gifts because we are reluctant to note and admit our need. Some of us are like the spiritually sufficient whom Jesus encountered. We have answers; we have no needs. So we bypass the joy and pain of spiritual growth.

However, I am grateful for people who have helped me experience the OKness of needing others. In light of that awareness, I thank God for the positive aspect which hopelessness affords. Why? Because it frees me to be open to new, undiscovered dimensions of hope that Jesus revealed.

Feelings of despair may not necessarily mean lack of faith. On the contrary, they may be the door to new spiritual insight or action, to new hope for our journey. Granted, when we experience conflict, we long for resolution. When we recognize our need for change, we renew hope through being open and vulnerable. When we know spiritual drought and are alert to spiritual nourishment, God's Spirit can come to us with living water like Jesus offered to the Samaritan woman.

I like the way John tells us about Jesus' encounter with the Samaritan woman. We get a fairly clear picture of Jesus' bringing hope to one whose life seemed hopeless, by that day's standard of morality. Jesus not only spoke to her; his very essence pulsed with and offered new life. In his presence she found acceptance and a new way of being for herself.

According to cultural and religious standards, the person spoken of in Chapter 4 has three bad labels. 1) She is a woman. To be a woman was not an honorable identity. 2) She is a Samaritan. Samaritans were despised by Jews. They were regarded with disdain. For example, Samaritan women were considered unclean from the day of their birth, with no hope of overcoming the plight. 3) She is an immoral person. Anyone guilty of any gross moral misdemeanour was scorned and ostracized from society.

The woman clearly lacked hope. Anyone relating to her could expect similar labels. Therefore, Jesus intentionally put himself in a precarious position by initiating conversation with her. He saw beyond all her

9

labels and reached out to the center of her very being with his love and concern.

Jesus' ministry, as outlined by all four Gospel writers, is one involving much risk-taking. Jesus chose to travel through Samaria on his way from Judea to Galilee. Jewish travellers intruding on Samaritan territory were frequently attacked. Jesus could have taken another route. Instead, Jesus took the risk of travelling the road where he could encounter difficulty. He took an even greater risk when he sent his disciples into town while he waited alone without any protection. But that risk he made into opportunity. While he waited, the Samaritan woman came to draw water.

Jesus spoke with her and broke all norms of Jewish-Samaritan communication. Since men were not even to look at women in public, let alone speak to them, his action could cripple his reputation. But Jesus ignored that. Here was someone experiencing hopelessness, toward whom Jesus reached out, offering to meed her need. And she received his message of hope because she was open and ready for it.

I suspect the woman may have known fear and anxiety. But it did not hinder her receptivity to a new message. In fact, it probably served as a creative force as she allowed herself the acceptance being offered her. Jesus made clear to his Jewish followers that a person they degraded qualified more than they as one who comprehended him. He restored in the Samaritan woman a sense of self worth and trusted her to take the hopeful word of redemption to her people.

God sent Jesus to reveal hope. Jesus revealed that hope through faithfulness in becoming human. What Jesus said and did cannot be separated from who he was. In his humanness he laughed, cried, played, learned, sorrowed and rejoiced, hoped and feared. Through such personality features God was manifested. In his interaction with people, Jesus brought hope to those in despair, healing to the sufferers, and sight to the blind. His exchange with people was not passive. In his meeting them, he took positive action. In his conversation with the Samaritan woman, he changed her enslavement to self and culture into a new freedom in the Spirit.

What does this story reveal to us today? We have already noted that Jesus brought hope to people as he related to them and met their needs. I believe that sometimes we minimize the relational impact we can have on each other as we share our common faith experience. I long for a revival among us. A revival which will free us to share our feelings of hopelessness and despair. A revival which will allow us to be real with each other. A revival which will infuse in us a spiritual hope beyond that which we could ever imagine.

I believe our hope is too narrowly defined. We hope for little and are not disappointed when we gain nothing. However, hope, as revealed by Jesus Christ, is as extensive as God. Anything can be expected without binding God in anyway. Hope depends on the premise that the Giver provides only what is good. Being totally unrestricted, hope finds expression through our openness to God's response. Someone has said that "Hope is the radical refusal to set limits to the goodness of God."

The kind of revival I long for is an openness to each other combined with a refusal to set limits on God's goodness. This is what I see demonstrated in Jesus' encounter with the Samaritan woman. In our commitment to follow Christ, we choose Jesus as our model and example of revealing hope. Are we willing to take the risk of bringing hope to each other? How will we respond to that challenge?

I am reminded of the chaplain who visited a young woman patient the evening before her major diagnostic surgery. She expressed her lack of faith and hope in God in these words. "If I could only believe that God will be with me tomorrow, then I would not need to be afraid of what the outcome will be." As she continued to express her hopelessness, the chaplain pondered how to best comfort her. Finally, the chaplain spoke: "Could you allow me to have the hope and faith you need as you enter surgery and until such a time as you find new hope within yourself?" The young woman grabbed the chaplain's hand and wept. Her own hope was restored over the next few weeks by the chaplain's willingness to risk in her behalf. Are we willing to put ourselves on the line for the sake of others? The chaplain could have chosen to avoid "Samaria"--the difficult encounter of responding to a hopeless plea. Instead, the risk of relating brought new hope.

I wonder who the Samaritans are today? Who are those for whom life seems hopeless? Where are those for whom life holds nothing but injustice? They may live next door, occupy the same pew as we, or perhaps even live in our own house. We as a people of faith who believe that our hope is in God through Jesus Christ share the responsibility to bring hope where there is despair, to correct injustices where they thrive, and to work toward achieving equality and liberation for all, regardless of sex, race, or creed. As we look around our world today, reasons abound for peoples' despair. We can choose to join the prophets of doom who see little hope and who predict only darkness. Or we can choose to extend the Christian hope we have within ourselves.

In conclusion let me share with you some words of Henri Nouwen about hope, words he in turn had quoted from an unidentified man.

> Hope means to keep living
> amid desperation
> and to keep humming
> in the darkness.
> Hope is knowing that there is love;
> it is trust in tomorrow;
> it is falling asleep
> and waking again
> when the sun rises.
> In the midst of a gale at sea,
> it is to discover land.
> In the eyes of another,
> it is to see that he understands you.
> ....
> Hope is recognizing that God

11

MARTHA SMITH GOOD

> As long as there is still hope
> There will also be prayer.
> ....
> And God will be holding you
> in his hands.   (p. 85, WITH OPEN HANDS)

MARTHA SMITH GOOD presented this teaching at the Mennonite Church Assembly
in 1981 at Bowling Green, Ohio. Martha is pastor of the Guelph Mennonite
Church in Ontario, having had previous pastoring assignments elsewhere.
(See the final sermon in this collection which was preached at her service
of commissioning.)

Promises to Keep
Anne Neufeld Rupp

We are graced in living on this side of the Incarnation, Crucifixion, Resurrection, and the coming of the Spirit. Thus, the joy, warmth and splendor of Christmas is not only a seasoned event. We have the privilege of experiencing this 365 days a year.

We are also graced in being given times in our life to evaluate, reflect, and reassess. Where are we in our Christian life? What are we doing? Where are we going? I believe that the week between Christmas Day and New Years Day gives us time for such reflection, re-newal and re--flection.

I want to guide our thoughts in that direction this morning, as we move towards the new year.

Once upon a time in a land far away where the waters run blue, and the earth rises to meet the sky, there lived a man who had two wives. The name of the man was Elkanah. And the man--though virtuous, of great lineage, and known through the land--was deeply disturbed at the disputes between his wives, the bitterness and the jealousy of the bickering women. Day after day he saw the rivalry between the two.

And little wonder, for it was a day and an age when women were defined by their ability to bear offspring. Failure to do so meant that the woman had little worth. Of the two wives, one bore sons and daughters while the other had borne none.

Hannah was deeply saddened, bitter, and hurt. She asked repeatedly: "What have I done to deserve this failure?" "What have I done to deserve this agony, this bitterness, this sense of lostness in being a woman?"

Although her husband would comfort her and say, "It is you I love, as you love me. Am I not worth more to you than ten sons?" The barren woman would turn away grieved in her heart and bitter still because the one wish of her life--that of having a son--had not been granted. Then the fruitful

13

Then the fruitful wife was prompted by jealousy as she saw Elkanah give more love to the barren one. In her spite she taunted and jeered Hannah. She carried her head just a little bit higher through the market place, and lifted her nose just a little bit more as she passed the unfortunate one. She indeed was a woman of worth, while the other was not.

Particularly when the yearly festival was celebrated, Elkanah noted the bitterness and hostility between the women. At that time of celebrative sacrifice, he granted a portion to each one who participated. To Peninnah he would grant a portion and to each of her children. To Hannah he could grant only one sacrificial portion. Suggesting that Hannah's worship was worth less, Peninnah would taunt her and say, "Ha, ha! Look! Look at all the sacrifices my children and I bring! And you bring only one." Hearing that, Hannah would weep and bow her head as though shamed. She had not accomplished the one great thing which a woman of that time should do. Elkanah would try again to comfort her and say, "I love you, my dear one; am I not worth to you more than ten sons?" But she wept--bitterly.

Year after year, as the time of the great sacrifice occurred, Hannah's head bent a little lower, while her shoulders became more stooped with the burden she was bearing. Her heart was heavy. Finally, she could bear it no more.

She went into the temple and in utter distress prayed to Yahweh. She writhed in agony; she lamented; she cried and sobbed. She implored the Great One, "Give me but a child. Give me that one thing that I most desire and I promise--I vow to you--that that child will be returned to you."

When the priest of the sacrifice observed the moaning and the groaning and the crying, he thought for certain that this woman must be drunk, totally deranged, or a woman of bad repute.

He turned, shook her by the shoulder, and said, "Woman! How shame you this place of sacrifice with such abominable behaviour?" Away with you! Fie! Shame! You have defiled this place of sacrifice!"

The woman looked up at him mournfully and said, "O, sir, I am not a drunkard. I am a woman so deeply bowed by sorrow that I am beside myself. I have begged of the Great One but one great gift, a son."

As the priest looked anew, he saw that indeed she was a good woman. Enlightened, he said, "Go in peace, my daughter. May the God of Israel grant your petition."

Hannah went her way, assured enough to eat and to sleep. Rest had come to her soul and peace to her mind. Although the taunts and jeers of Peninnah persisted, the irritations being like lashes on her back, Hannah carried a hope like a lamp in her heart.

Following a final worship event, the household of Elkanah returned to their village. And following intimacy in which Yahweh remembered the earnestness of Hannah, new life emerged. Days fled into weeks and weeks into months. We can imagine that early one morning, as dawn streaked silver fingers into the sky and awakening birds sang their melodies into the fresh cool air, a son was born. And the mother looked upon him fondly saying,

"You are a gift, and I have a promise to keep."

She cared for and nursed the child, and when he was old enough, she took him back to the place of sacrifice. Worshipping Yahweh--rejoicing in salvation that was hers--she said, "Eli, I Hannah, am the one you observed several years ago praying to Yahweh. Yahweh has been good, so I have a promise to keep. I hereby give my child to Yahweh." And her heart was glad.

The story of Elkanah, Hannah, and their child Samuel--later to become the prophet Samual--is found in First Samuel, chapter 1. This story tells of a God who encounters people through their common experience. God works with long range goals. Samuel came to have a place in God's history and plan. God continues to shape purposes, working through people: men, women, youth, and children. Through you and me.

This story is one of promise, promise made and promise kept. Such stories have made all the difference within Old Testament history. Are you conscious of how the promises we make and break change history? When vows or agreements are so easily made and broken, we do well to think about promise. The familiar phrase "Promise her anything" suggests a very shallow understanding. Promise made only for the sake of getting what we want prior to breaking off the relationship fails to comprehend authentic relationship--with God or others.

We all have made promises.

1) Do you remember when you committed your life to Jesus Christ? In that act of saying, "I will follow Jesus," you made promises: to put Jesus Christ first in your life, to take his teachings seriously, to serve him with your whole being--your mind, body, and spirit. Have you kept that promise?

2) Do you remember the day of your baptism? Understanding the implications of discipleship, you made a promise to study God's word. Your intent was to become familiar with the meaning of being a follower. You promised to be a discipled Christian, a disciplined Christian, and a Christ-oriented person growing in the knowledge of Jesus Christ, in finding favor with God. Your intent was to grow spiritually in wisdom and in stature. Have you kept your promise?

3) And do you remember your commitment to be a member of the church? In that, you promised to give of yourself, not only to God but to the church of which Jesus Christ is the source, with each member contributing a part. In that, you promised to participate within the body, to be available, to share and to care because you saw yourself as a steward of your talents, time, and money. Have you kept your promise?

There also are other promises. Some spoken, some unspoken. Promises you made on your wedding day for your marriage. Promises you made with your family--to your parents, your children. What happened, what has resulted through those promises?

Or, there are other significant times in our lives. Perhaps, like Hannah, you have been in deep pain and have said to God, "God, I promise you if only you will...." Then often in looking back to such occasions, we acknowledge God's faithfulness, but have we proven consistent? How have

we kept our promises? How have our promises, and the way they've been forgotten or kept, affected the course of God's history? Where are we in our
Christian journey? What are we doing about keeping faith strong?

A poem by Robert Frost suggests "I have promises to keep and miles to
go before I sleep." We have a week of miles ahead of us. A week in which
to reflect on our promises. A week in which to correct, adapt, and in-
tensify our patterns of responding. A week in which to also make new promises. Promises to keep.

Amen.

ANNE NEUFELD RUPP preached this in the Sunday morning worship service at
Alexanderwohl Mennonite Church on December 26, 1982. She co-pastors this
General Conference congregation with her husband Kenneth. Anne was or-
dained in 1976.

Joy — A Quality of the Spirit
Norma J. Johnson

Scripture: Phil. 4:4-13

The Theme of joy is evident in this passage of Paul's to the Philippians. One biblical scholar indicates that the word joy is used sixty times in the New Testament and the word rejoice appears seventy two times. The index of The Mennonite Hymnal lists approximately sixty hymns in the joy section.

Jesus talked about joy in John 15:11. This verse follows the section where he's been talking about the vine and the branches. He says, "I have told you this so that my joy may be in you and that your joy may be complete." Paul commends joy in his letter to the Thessalonians. "Be joyful always." (5:16) Paul prayed with joy at the beginning of the letter to the Philippians because of their partnership with him in the gospel. The theme of joy continues throughout the book. The Layman's Bible Commentary suggests:

> What then are the aspects of Paul's many-sided character which
> shine out clearest in Philippians? In the first place must
> surely go his unquenchable Christian serenity and joy. "I re-
> joice and you must rejoice too" which, though he writes from
> prison, is the theme of many of his exhortations. Better than
> any of his other letters, Philippians exemplifies the truth of
> the statement that God's best servants have never been sad peo-
> ple. That through all trials and tribulations, Christian cheer-
> fulness has a way of breaking in.

Another familiar passage that notes joy is Gal. 5:22-23, where the fruits of the spirit are identified. "But the fruit of the spirit is love, joy, peace, patience, kindness, goodness, faithfulness, gentleness, and self-control." J. B. Philips' translation begins: "The spirit, however, produces in human life fruits such as these . . . ." I believe he tells us plainly that these are to be qualities observable in our daily life here and now. The fruits of the spirit are not for some grand day off in the future. When Paul lists the fruits of the spirit, he doesn't indicate that some of us will be cheerful, some patient, some peaceful, some gentle, etc. Not optional, these are to be found in all our lives. Concerning the gifts of the spirit, some will have particular gifts while others have different ones. But no footnote in scripture tells us that we are to cultivate only one or two of the fruits of the spirit.

Countless authors have written extensively on the subject of joy. In his book, Spirit Fruit, John M. Drescher wrote:

> Joy is love smiling. It is love exalting, rejoicing; the echo of pleasant words of love we speak to others and the overflow of happiness we give to others because we have happiness deep within. It's dependent on a relationship to Jesus Christ. It is the inward reality which produces outward radiance.

Richard J. Foster, a Quaker author, says this about joy in his book Celebration of Discipline:

> Often I'm inclined to think that joy is like a motor, the thing that keeps everything else going. Without joyous celebration to infuse the other spiritual disciplines, we will sooner or later abandon them. Joy produces energy. Joy makes us strong.

Joy indeed energized Maria van Beckum and her sister-in-law, Ursula, two Anabaptist martyrs whose story is told in Martyrs Mirror. The theme of joy came through their life in spite of the hardship and the suffering they faced.

In 1544 Maria became an Anabaptist. Her mother made her leave home because of this, so Maria went to live with her brother John and his wife, Ursula. The authorities discovered where Maria was, and late one night a large group appeared at the house to arrest her. Maria was frightened and asked Ursula to go with her to keep her company. John agreed and Ursula's reply was, "If John is satisfied, I will gladly go with you and we will rejoice together in the Lord."

The two women were first taken to Deventer where they were questioned at length by the officials. Later, they were moved to Delden where additional authorities, some from the church and some from the courts, questioned them. Maria and Ursula quoted scripture to support their views and refused to recant. On November 13, 1544, in the open court at Delden they were sentenced to death. As their sentence was announced, they rejoiced and praised God. While watching them being led to the stake, many people, on seeing their steadfastness, wept. They sang for joy and said, "Weep not on account of what is inflicted on us; we do not suffer as witches or other criminals, but because we adhere to Christ, and we will not be separated from God."

Adelaide Ann Procter, a woman who lived from 1825-1864, also had this quality of joy in her life. She's the writer of the text of the hymn "My God, I Thank Thee." Adelaide was born in England, the daughter of the poet Brian Waller Procter who wrote under the pen name Barry Cornwall. Charles

Dickens was a close friend of the Procter family. Adelaide wrote poetry and submitted it to the literary magazine "Household Words" which Dickens edited. However, she always submitted her poetry under the name Mary Berwick, because she was afraid if Dickens knew her identity, he would publish her work because of family friendship rather than because of quality.

Adelaide converted to Roman Catholicism in 1861 and gave herself up to working for the poor. She did this so enthusiastically that she ruined her health and at one point was bedridden for fifteen months. Though a frail, sickly person, she was always cheerful and vivacious, even during illness. Adelaide died when 39. Having known well the suffering of illness, she nevertheless was triumphant in soul. Her habitual cheery disposition and buoyant sense of humor shine through her poems. The hymn, "My God, I Thank Thee," written in 1858, uses Psalms 104:24 as its basis. "Countless are the things thou hast made, oh Lord; thou hast made all by thy wisdom. And the earth is full of thy creatures."

> (Note to reader: At this point in the sermon we sang this hymn. The congregation paused after each verse and at that point I shared with them some ways in which this hymn has become meaningful to me. We spent time in silence pondering and reflecting on the words of each verse. Then I read a scripture verse and we sang the next stanza.)

"My God, I Thank Thee" (# 267 in The Mennonite Hymnal)
Think of the theme of joy that comes through these words written by Adelaide Ann Procter.

> v. 1: My God, I thank Thee, who has made
>   The earth so bright,
>   So full of splendor and of joy, beauty and light.
>   So many glorious things are here, noble and right.

Desert flowers in bloom . . . a sunrise at the ocean. . . colored leaves . . . drifting snow. . . rugged mountains. . . tea in a favorite mug. . . a flickering bayberry candle. . . birthday celebrations. . . the spontaneity and enthusiasm of children.

> Ponder the glorious things that are noble and right.

> v. 2: I thank Thee, too, that Thou hast made
>   Joy to abound,
>   So many gentle thoughts and deeds circling us round;
>   That in the darkest spot of earth
>   Some love is found.

Sharing a meal in a student's village hut. . . the writings of Henri Nouwen and Madeleine L'Engle. . . taking a journaling workshop. . . a letter from a good friend. . . meaningful work. . . friends that drop by unexpectedly.

> Ponder the gentle thoughts and deeds circling us round.

> Col. 1:11: "May he strengthen you in his glorious might with ample power to meet whatever comes with fortitude, patience, and joy."

> v. 3: I thank Thee more that all our joy
>   Is touched with pain;
>   That shadows fall on brightest hours
>   That thorns remain,

> So that earth's bliss may be our guide,
> And not our chain.

An empty mailbox. . . a truck accident. . . hectic schedules. . .my
mother's nervous breakdown. . . cancer. . .my dad's heart attack. . .
waiting. . . more waiting.

> Ponder the way pain intersects the joy in our life.
> Psalms 30:5: "Tears may linger at nightfall, but joy comes in the
>   morning."
> Psalms 107:43: "Ponder the record of the Lord's enduring love."
> v. 4: I thank Thee, Lord, that Thou has kept
>   The best in store;
>   We have enough, yet not too much
>   To long for more,
>   A yearning for a deeper peace
>   Not known before. Amen.

Enjoying the now. . . pondering the future. . . considering the options. .
. confident in God's leading.

> Reflect a bit on what God does have in store.
> II Cor. 4:18: "Meanwhile, our eyes are fixed, not on the things that
>   are seen, but on the things that are unseen, for what is seen
>   passes away; what is unseen is eternal."

Let us pray.

O God, we pray for strength and courage to be joyful servants. We confess
to you the times in our lives when we were not joyful. Grant to each of
us an openness to the work of the Spirit in our lives so that love and joy
will be qualities evident to those around us. We thank you for examples
of joy in the lives of the apostle Paul, the Anabaptist women Maria and
Ursula, and the hymnwriter Adelaide. Amen.

NORMA J. JOHNSON preached this sermon at Akron Mennonite Church, Akron, Pa.
on August 22, 1982. Norma is on the pastoral team there and also works in
personnel services, as Director, at MCC (Mennonite Central Committee) having completed several assignments in Kenya and Botswana.

Dance in Worship
Priscilla Stuckey Kauffman

To meditate with you on the theme of dance in worship, I could begin by describing to you all the functions that dance can fulfill in worship, such as a tool for teaching, or an accompaniment to singing. Or I could begin by listing all the places in the Old Testament where dance is men- tioned as a part of Hebrew worship. But I do not want to talk about how useful dance can be in worship, as if it only serves some of the more ver- bal parts of the service. Neither do I want us to dance in worship simply because that's what was done in Bible times or because there happens to be a good tradition behind it. Usefulness and tradition are not sufficient to describe what I see is the primary importance of dance, among others arts, in worship.

I would like to speak of dance and the arts in a more fundamental way: as expressions of our joy in being created earthy, worldy beings who are nevertheless co-creators in the image of God. I want to speak of the arts as expressions of our delight in all the sensory pleasures bestowed upon us earthcreatures: pleasures of sight, smell, taste, hearing, and touch.

I want us to see the arts as expressive of our human love for the world, our response to that extravagant love which God Herself showed to the world in the birthing process of creation. As God's love for the world initiated the creative process, so perhaps our love for the world assists God in the process of recreation.

From Genesis 1:

In the beginning God created the heavens and the earth.
Now the earth was formless and empty;
Darkness was over the face of the deep,
And the Spirit of God was hovering over the waters

And God said, "Let there be light," and there was light.
God saw that the light was good,

And God separated light from the darkness.
And there was evening and there was morning--the first day.

And God said, "Let there be an expanse between the waters."
And it was so. God called the expanse, "sky."
And there was evening, and there was morning--the second day.

And God said, "Let the water under the sky be gathered to one place,
And let dry ground appear." And it was so.
And God saw that it was good.

Then God said, "Let the land produce vegetation."
And it was so. The land produced vegetation, according to their
    various kinds.
And God saw that it was good.
And there was evening, and there was morning--the third day.

And God said, "Let there be lights in the expanse of the sky,
    to separate the day from night, to mark seasons and days
    and years, and to give light on the earth."
And it was so. God made two great lights--and God saw that it was
    good.
And there was evening, and there was morning--the fourth day.

And God said, "Let the water teem with living creatures,
    and let birds fly above the earth."
So God created every moving thing with which the water teems,
    and every winged bird.
And God saw that it was good.
And there was evening, and there was morning--the firth day.

And God said, "Let the land produce living creatures."
And it was so. God made the wild animals, the livestock,
    and all the creatures that move along the ground.
And God saw that it was good.

Then God said, "Let us make humankind in our image, in our likeness."
So God created humankind in his own image,
In the image of God he created him,
Male and female he created them.

God saw all that he had made, and it was <u>very</u> good.
And there was evening, and there was morning--the sixth day.

Thus the heavens and the earth were completed <u>in all their vastness</u>.

We have here a picture of a creation full of sensory delights: of a
velvet plant's fuzzy, purple leaves; of honey that's sticky and sweet; of
mud in all its slurpy gooiness; of a giraffe's soft brown eyes and long,
spotted neck; of the joy of human touch and sexual companionship. They
are all here in this vision of a splendidly diversified creation laughing
together, cavorting together on the morning of its birth.

"And God saw that it was good."

The Genesis 1 vision of a magnificent created order is only part of the picture we live with, however. On a vast scale we are conscious of the incompleteness and imperfection of the created order. Genesis 2 and 3, the other creation story, tells about the fall, in an attempt to understand the pain and injustices which seem to characterize so much of life.

Our Western Christian tradition also participates in this fallenness. We are inheritors of traditions which speak, not of wholeness and harmony, but of all the separations and divisions which are part of our view of the world. The Greeks, for instance, made much of the idea that the spirit and the body are opposed to one another, and that the things of the spirit are superior to the things of the body. The spiritual realm is the most real one, the eternal one; the earthly realm is the imperfect, evil arena.

But as if that division were not enough to severely complicate life, they went a step further and identified the qualities of the two realms with differences between men and women. Man was the personification of all those higher qualities of intellect, spiritual immortality, and objective experience, while woman personified all the lower qualities of bodiliness, mortality, sensuality, and subjective experience. Woman was the very image of all that dragged man away from a higher spiritual existence.

These ideas were absorbed into Christianity through some of the Church Fathers of the first five centuries. Some pictured woman as the image of evil temptation; these blamed her for the very fall of creation. They interpreted true spirituality as trying to escape from the mortal body into the immortality of the spirit by denying the body its wants and needs. In some cases this meant forbidding contact with women, and in most cases, it meant that man, with his spiritual wisdom, was supposed to dominate the evil earthiness of woman.

The Anabaptists also inherited this separation of spirit and body. But this dualism was not the only one they felt. They took seriously the reality of fallenness, and they held central those parts of the New Testament which call for a clear distinction between the ways of the world and the ways of Jesus' followers. They quoted Paul's admonition to "Be not conformed to this world," and the advice of James , chapter 1, that "Pure, undefiled service of God is to keep oneself unspotted from the world." They interpreted "the world" to be everything outside the community of obedient believers. For the Anabaptists, there were only two types of people in the world: believers and unbelievers, or those who have come out of the world and those who remain in it.

Strict rules of conduct separated the church from the world, and some of these rules dealt with the use of the arts. A portion of a confession of faith written by Peter Rideman in 1540 illustrates this. Rideman became the leader of the Hutterite movement, but he also represents much of early Anabaptist thought. The section quoted comes from "Concerning Singing," which builds on the text in Ephesians and Colossians which reads, "Sing and make melody in your heart to the Lord, with psalms and hymns and spiritual songs."

(To sing) in the right way (is to sing) attentively, in the
fear of God, and as inspired by the Spirit 6f Christ....(When)
one singeth only for carnal joy or for the sweet sound or for
some such reason,...one misuseth (the spiritual songs), changing them into what is carnal and worldly....Likewise also, he
who enjoyeth listening for the music's sake...sinneth greatly
against God; for he useth his word, which was given for his
salvation, as leading him to the lust of the flesh and to sin.
(Peter Rideman, Confession of Faith, Holder and Stoughton, 1950, p. 123.)

This statement is a harsh treatment of the arts and of the normal
human sensory and artistic pleasures. I include it, not so that we may
pass judgment on Peter Rideman, but so that we understand more clearly that
part of our tradition.

Each of these divisions--the separation of the body from the spirit,
the separation of the church from the world--results from that deeper alienation that affects us all: the incompleteness, the imperfection of the
whole created order in which we share. Yet, we as Christians believe that
in the life, death, and resurrection of Jesus, God was giving us a sign
intended to complete that process of creation begun in Genesis 1. We speak
of Jesus as the firstborn of all the children, the firstfruit of the new
creation, the sign that more is to follow. Each of the events of Jesus'
life, death, and resurrection is a sign that God's love is indeed shown to
this created order.

Jesus was, first of all, a human being, and he participated in all the
sights, sounds, feelings, and limitations common to human life. Finally,
he experienced that one event which, more than any other, marks our human
limitedness: Jesus died. But then the unheard-of happened: Jesus was also
raised from death!

The story the gospel writers tell is not one of immortality. They do
not speak of Jesus' being freed from his body and going off into some bliss-
ful spiritual eternity. No, the language they use to describe the mysterious event of Jesus' renewed life is language of resurrection. They speak
of his coming back to some form of earthly life. Exactly what sort of form,
what kind of body he had, they do not elaborate. But they agree that he
was not purely spirit. He was a resurrected person, "The firstfruits of
all who have fallen asleep," says Paul (I Cor. 15:20).

Taken seriously, the resurrection of Jesus gives us a profound hope
for what God's love intends for the whole created order. This cosmic vision for the fulfillment of the whole creation, for reconciliation on a
grand scale, was part of Paul's hope for the future. I think of the passage in Romans 8 which speaks of the whole creation groaning as it awaits
liberation from its bondage to decay.

I think that what we suffer in this life can never be compared
to the glory, as yet unrevealed, which is waiting for us. The
whole creation is eagerly waiting for God to reveal his sons.
It was not for any fault on the part of creation that it was
made unable to attain its purpose, it was made so by God; but
creation still retains the hope of being freed, like us, from

24

its slavery to decadence, to enjoy the same freedom and glory as the children of God. From the beginning till now the entire creation, as we know, has been groaning in one great act of giving birth; and not only creation, but all of us who possess the first fruits of the Spirit, we too groan inwardly as we wait for our bodies to be set free. (Romans 8:18-23)

Paul's vision here includes the image of creation waiting for its resurrected body, as we wait for ours. God, the expectant mother, still struggles to bring the new creation to birth.

This period of waiting in hope is the tension we feel between the present and the future: between the present time, in which we know both decay and foretastes of glory, and the future, when God will complete the process of reconciling the world to the Divine. This is the tension between experiencing the firstfruits of the Spirit without the satisfaction of the whole harvest. I do not experience this very gently. It tugs at the very center of my being and speaks to my deepest desires.

This vision of the whole created order renewed into its full glory brings tears to my eyes each time I submit myself to its images. It confronts me in all of life's activities and reminds me that this world has not arrived at glory. I long for that final feast of heaven, when tables shall be turned and wrongs made right, when men and women and all of creation will be reconciled into that harmony and partnership for which they were intended.

An Episcopal priest, Robert Farrar Capon, wrote a theological cookbook Supper of the Lamb in which he describes this longing. He speaks of it as "the greater heartburn," the type of heartburn that can't be cured with baking soda or Rolaids. He calls this pain

the higher distress for which earth has no cure--that major, vaster burning by which the heart looks out astonished at the world, and, in its loving, wakes and breaks at once....For all its greatness, the created order cries out for further greatness still....We embrace the world in all its glorious solidity, yet it struggles in our very arms, and declares itself a pilgrim world....Why do we marry, why take friends and lovers, why give ourselves to music, painting, chemistry, or cooking? Out of simple delight in the goodness of creation, of course, but out of more than that, too. Half of the earth's gorgeousness lies rooted in the glimpsed city it longs to become. For all its loveliness, the world has no continuing city here; and it is our glory to see it so and thirst until Jerusalem comes home at last. We were given appetites, not to consume the world and forget it, but to taste its goodness and long to make it great. That is the unconsolable heartburn, the lifelong disquietude of having been made in the image of God.

Capon explains that the way we image God is in our love for the world and our longing to see it re-created. He suggests that human activities which spring from our love of the world are part of what will make possible God's completion of the redemptive process.

I believe, with Capon, that our participation in the arts can be one expression of our love for the world, one of those human activities that can assist God in the re-creation of the world. I believe this happens in two ways.

First of all, in recalling Genesis 1, I see our acceptance of the arts as our acceptance of creatureliness. The arts, above all, appeal unashamedly to all of our sensory perceptors, as did the picture of the created order painted in Genesis 1. Peter Rideman and other Anabaptists were only too aware of this fact. The arts are the expressions of body people making use of every sound and every feel that they are privileged to produce. In the arts we do not deny the pleasures and abilities afforded us as earth creatures. Rather, we accept them as gifts from the Creator, and we seek to enjoy them in the context of the goodness for which they were intended.

Perhaps, in our artistic expressions of our love for the world, we become co-creators with God in the unveiling of the new creation. Perhaps in the very act of accepting ourselves as creatures, we are given the power to become creators also. Perhaps this one form of our love for the world patterns something of God's love shown in the creative process, and something of Jesus' love in living, dying, and being resurrected on this earth. And, perhaps, in this way our love participates in bringing about the new order.

What then of a dance group in worship? Dance is that one form of the arts with which we have felt especially uncomfortable. It's the most blatantly bodily form of all the arts. For the dancers it involves moving our bodies and feeling kinship with the bodies of other dancers. For the congregation, it means watching bodies move. In most of Assembly's tradition this has meant watching female bodies, bodies which have long been considered the source of temptation to men.

I believe accepting God's love for the world (as we see it in the creative and redemptive processes) means that we let go of the belief that bodies (female or male) represent that side of life which must be dominated by the mind or spirit. It means being willing to call our bodies ourselves--the way we would call our personalities ourselves--instead of seeing our bodies merely as the instruments or tools of our minds. Accepting God's love for the world means we accept and rejoice in both bodily and spiritual parts of our personhood. It means, finally, accepting our mortality as a fact of our earthly existence, without trying to escape from it by denying bodily life. God loves us in this world, and while we remain here, we are privileged to receive that love in and through our bodiliness. In this way we are free to value dance in worship, because our bodies are integral to understanding the meaning of being creatures in relationship with their Creator.

In conclusion, the dance group would like to interpret the story of the raising of Lazarus told in John 11. I would invite you to join in as villagers witnessing the event, watching Jesus share a foretaste of fulfillment.

PRISCILLA STUCKEY KAUFFMAN presented this teaching for Community and Campus clusters of Assembly Mennonite Church, Goshen, Indiana on September 27, 1981 and October 4, 1981. Priscilla will enter the Pacific School of Religion in historical studies this coming fall.

We are God's Work of Art
Sue Richard

Ephesians 2:1-10
Hymn # 426 - <u>The Mennonite Hymnal</u>

(In keeping with the theme, I prepared a display on the communion table.
On one side of the table was an old tub with three or four lumps of potter's
clay in it, and on the other were four or five different shaped pieces of
pottery. This I used in telling the concluding story or parable, which
story was particularly for the children present.)

Two years ago the members of Shiroishi Mennonite church in Sappore,
Japan decided to observe a Culture Day Sunday. Culture Day is a national
holiday in November. Culture Sunday was planned for Sunday of the week of
Culture Day. For that special day, children brought in art works and projects from school. Women brought garden products, needle work, and other
homemade articles. People brought Japanese calligraphy works, oil paint-
ings, poems, and songs for display in the sanctuary. The objects ranged
from simple, small articles to large, impressive works. Quite an array.
Why did we have a Culture Sunday? We wanted to get better acquainted
with the gifts and talents among us. Once aware of the diversity of gifts
within the congregation, we could more easily tap latent talents for the
congregation's use. This proved to be a comfortable way for reserved people to declare their abilities.
In this message, I'd like us to think about the fact that we are God's
work of art. We will look at more than one image. In our text, Eph. 2:10,
we are likened to a poem. In Japanese we would say we are God's <u>kessaku,</u>
the culmination of all that was created. We are God's masterpiece or the
zenith of all creativity.
I already mentioned that in Japan we observe Culture Day. While there,
I tried to find out when and why Culture Day began. I asked friends,

checked encyclopedias, and read through Japanese books, but I was unable
to find adequate information. I think that Culture Day began during the
Meiji era when the Japanese began to develop self-consciousness in relation to other nations, when they wanted to advance their culture. Until
that time they were an isolated nation.

But my focus today is not Japan's Culture Day. I want us to think
about when God's Culture Day began. When was the first culture day?
Where would we go to find out about the beginnings of culture? While the
Japanese would turn to their ancient manuscript, the KOJIKI, and its creation story crediting the sun god and goddess, we will turn to the Bible
to read about creation and the beginning of culture.

When we do so, we do well to remember that early Genesis material is
not a historical account of events. It suggests a spiritual account of
salvation history. The very first words of our book portray the setting
before there was culture or a civilization or even a world. Gen. 1:2 says
"the earth was without form and void, and darkness was upon the face of
the deep." We have difficulty imagining the blackness or the emptiness of
space. We need word pictures to help us understand. James Weldon Johnson,
a little-known black poet, used vivid word pictures in his poem "The Creation."

    And as far as the eye of God could see
    Darkness covered everything
    Blacker than a hundred midnights
    Down in a cypress swamp.

    Then God smiled and the light broke
    And the darkness rolled up on one side
    And the light stood shining on the other
    And God said, "That's good."

The first pages of Scripture begin with God's creative acts. "In the
beginning God created the heavens and the earth." The story tells the sequence of six creation days. After each creation day, God reflected on
the work, as a true artist does. "And God saw that it was good."

We note, however, that the Master Artist didn't use tools. What
tool would you use to fashion the heavens and the earth, or to place the
stars and moon in their orbit? We need brushes, pens, or carving instruments, plus skilled hands to create. Even then, some of us are clumsy.
But the Master Designer spoke. That sounds incredible, doesn't it? Ponder
the thought. See if you gain a greater appreciation for the majesty and
greatness of the Great "I AM," the One who causes to be.

Picasso was also a great artist, one of the greatest of our century.
If you go to Chicago and visit the Art Museum on Michigan Avenue, you'll
see a number of his works. Picasso is noted for his "overwhelming quan-
tity of production....In 1953 Picasso produced 180 finished drawings in
nine weeks...but his works were often lacking in discrimination and good
taste." That remark will never describe the Master Artist who is still
creating and recreating.

In order to view God's masterpiece from a different perspective, consider Psalm 139:13-18. Creation activity is not haphazard. It has been intricately planned and carefully designed, reflecting the work of a Master mind. The Psalmist compares it to the work of a skilled craftsman who uses a needle and creates a design on a piece of tapestry. During the Psalmist's time beautiful, intricate embroidery work was woven into the high priest's gown or the curtain of the tabernacle. Then they were dedicated to the service of the sanctuary.

I think I understand the Psalmist's analogy a little better after examining a handmade piece of needle work recently. One of the members of our church showed us the embroidery work she received from a refugee woman of the family supported by the congregation. Mrs. Vang pulled single strands of silk thread from a garment she brought with her from Thailand to embroider a design on cloth. She designed as she stitched, a flawless, minutely designed piece of handiwork.

Is any one suffering from low self-esteem or a low self-image? Then study this passage and write your own psalm, if you feel moved. Take notice of the painstaking care God gave to our development during pregnancy. All nine months were under Divine watchfulness. The Psalmist doesn't end with a dirge of complaint "You've surely made a mistake, Yahweh, to create such an anamoly as myself." No, he bursts forth in praise. "It's all too wonderful for me. And the most comforting thought is of God's continuing presence.

Psalm 139 is like an art museum entered to view our Master Designer's work. Genesis 1 is one museum; Psalm 139 is another. Let's consider a third. But first, let's return to the question, when did culture begin? Culture first began in the Garden of Eden. We don't know much about the culture of the Garden--what types of patterns people had for carrying on their daily activities or how elaborately it was developed. But we do know it deteriorated since; perfection ceased. That was because of sin.

Because of sin, a second creation became necessary. This, Paul speaks about in Eph. 2. The same message appears in Isaiah 64. Isaiah presents a great historical museum. The picture painted is like an impressionistic work of art, almost like an abstract piece. It doesn't resemble the art of the Renaissance period when objects were reproduced as accurately as possible. Isaiah's word pictures reflect his incomplete understanding of the new creation. I'll read from the Good News translation, verses 6-7.

> All of us have been sinful, even our best actions are filthy
> through and through;
> Because of our sins we are like leaves that wither and are blown
> away by the wind.
> No one turns to you in prayer, no one goes to you for help;
> You have hidden yourself from us and have abandoned us because
> of our sins.

If we read this passage only one time, we'll consider it to be like abstract art, difficult to understand. But if we spend time in the passage and read it repeatedly, we'll discover its symetrical beauty. Its hidden message begins to emerge. We see that Isaiah's spiritual termi-

nology compares to the Genesis state of affairs before the creation.
There are important parallels in the two passages. Genesis suggests
"darkness covered everything." Isaiah says that before the new creation
they were or we are unclean, polluted, like dead leaves, formless. The
most dismal, dark description occurs at the end of verse 7. "You hid your
face from us."

Perhaps the best way to conceptualize the broken relationship with
God is to picture astronauts orbiting the moon. Everytime they come to
the back side of the moon, all communication lines are cut off. They
travel in total blackness until they come to the lighted side again. That
is what we experience when we are away from God; it's the most miserable
state we can know. But then, like brightness in the middle of a dark can-
vas, verse 8 offers stark relief. The Master Creator comes to our rescue.

Here the imagery of a potter and clay is used. Our Maker, Creator,
or Potter comes to a new creation. We should spend hours in this great
museum examining the theme of beginning. Take time also to look into
chapter 65, verses 17 and 18, for Isaiah's declaration about creating new
heavens and a new Jerusalem.

Our forth and final museum is Ephesians 2. Compare this to a museum
of Modern Art. Because of New Testament understanding, the lines, color,
and tone all seem to be richer, brighter, and clearer. Our Eph. 2:10
text states: "We are God's work of art." We are God's poem. As an exhi-
bit of our Creator, we are aesthetically beautiful and functionally useful, truly the artistic expression of our Maker.

One commentator suggests that "A true poem is so rare a thing, it
has always been appraised as the highest form of literature." Paul says
we are the expression of the mind of God. The intimacies of God's heart--
high thoughts and deep emotions--are expressed in man and woman. Another
writer says "The true Christian is God's poem in a world of prose; God's
beauty in a world of gloom; God's fine and finished art in a world where
people forget beauty and are careless of amoral symmetry and spiritual
grace." Doesn't that give dignity to our existence as Christians, whether
we're likened to a potter's vessel or a poem?

Paul gives us a clear picture of God's new creation. How does it take
place?--through Jesus Christ. And for what purpose?--for good works. At
the beginning of chapter 2, Paul, in very graphic language--like bold
strokes of a brush--uses descriptive word pictures to tell us why the new
creation was necessary. Then, with similar boldness mixed with warmth of
tone and richness of color, he gives us an equally vivid description of
what the new creation accomplishes. "He made us alive, raised us up, and
made us to sit with him in heavenly places."

Maybe you are thinking this isn't the "typical" missionary sermon. I
close with a parable, especially for the children. It's a parable that I
believe contains the missionary message for each one of us.

"Parable of the Little Lump of Clay" - By Arland Esch

Once upon a time there was a little lump of clay sitting in a tub
among other lumps of clay in the house of the great potter. This little

lump of clay had been rescued from the miry pits of the potter, who had brought him to his own house.

As the little lump of clay sat, he wondered to himself, what does the potter want me to be? He surely didn't bring me here just to sit in this tub. There must be some good reason for me to be here. So he looked a- round the house and saw shelves lined with beautiful pots, which were the work of the potter. The little lump of clay then said to himself, "Aha! I will be like one of those pots, curved with smooth lines and useful to the potter."

So the little lump of clay tried and tried and tried, but his form would not change. In desperation he cried out, "Help me! I don't want to be a lump forever!"

The potter, who was always near, heard his cry and reached down and rescued him from the tub. He set the lump on his workbench and began to mold and press him down to remove those vain empty spaces. The little lump cried out in pain, but he knew it was better than the stagnant old tub, for the potter's hands gently enveloped him. Excitement filled the little lump as the potter began to shape him into a beautiful pot like the ones on the shelves.

Then he looked down at the other lumps in the tub and said to himself, "poor suckers! How much better-looking am I than they! Why, if they had done as I had, they would not have to be ugly old lumps in a tub. Boast- fully, he looked down at himself. He was aghast. He cried out to the potter, "Wait! These are not the beautiful curves and smooth lines I want. This is nothing like those other pots you have made. You're making a big mistake."

So the little lump resisted the potter's gentle hands and began to make his own shape. But the more he tried to make beautiful curves and smooth lines, the more lopsided he became, until, with a great sigh, he fell into a heap and once again was a lump. The potter sadly picked him up and placed him back in the tub.

Despair came over the little lump of clay, and in desperation he cried out again to the potter, "Help me! I don't want to be a useless old lump forever." The potter, hearing his cry, reached down and drew him out. He set him on his worktable and again began to mold and shape the little lump of clay into a vessel fit for display in the house of the potter.

The little lump no longer looked down upon the other lumps in the tub, nor boastfully at himself, but kept his eyes steadfastly on the potter and said, "I delight to do your will." And the little lump of clay became a uniquely beautiful and useful pot in the house of the potter.

(Editor's note: I trust we will read this using female pronouns for the potter also.)

SUE RICHARD, having returned from 15 years in Japan as an English teacher missionary, now lives in Lombard, Illinois. She gave this sermon at First Mennonite Church in Iowa City, Iowa, on March 13, 1983.

Gifts of the Spirit . . . to Us
Ruth Brunk Stoltzfus

Scripture Reading: I Cor. 12:1-30

In I Cor. 12:1-30 the Apostle Paul writes about spiritual gifts and how they have something to do with us.

In the preceding chapters he dealt with problems of Christian faith and life that had arisen in the church he had established at Corinth. Corinth was that most important city of Greece known for its commerce, culture, immorality, and religions. The problems Paul spoke to were factions in the church, sexual immorality, problems in family life, Christian and pagan relations, lawsuits among believers.

In between the problems, and even in the midst of them, is gem after bright gem of spiritual truth. These include the cross of Christ and its power; the Spirit of God as the source of spiritual wisdom, understanding and power for the believer; and instruction for those who pray and proclaim God's message--men and women.

Noting the situation that some in the church follow Paul while others follow Apollos, Paul said, "What, after all, is Apollos?   And what is Paul?" They are servants, through whom you came to believe (I Cor. 3:5). Each servant functions with a portion of the task God had assigned, the task God further implements.

This is the concept we must keep in mind as we come to the question of spiritual gifts: We are servants to whom God has assigned individual tasks within corporate endeavor.

The Plan. What is the plan for receiving and using spiritual gifts in the life of the church? First of all to declare "Jesus is Lord." No one can really say that "except by the Holy Spirit" (I Cor. 12:3). To believers in Christ the Spirit gives gifts to be used in the church and its mission. To those dependent on self or other idols enthroned in their lives God's Spirit does not reveal truth.

The Spirit facilitates differing gifts. Men's gifts are not all a-like and women's gifts are not all alike. Therefore, we must not place men or women in frozen roles. Breaking the rigid and long-held Jewish custom in which rabbis refused to teach women, Jesus strongly affirmed Mary who was different from her own sister. She was validated in concentrating on kingdom work instead of kitchen work, as she sat at Jesus' feet listening and learning. "There are different kinds of gifts, but the same Spirit. There are different kinds of service, but the same God." (I Cor. 12:4-5)

Having differing gifts is essential for fulness of functioning within the church. Suppose everyone in the church had only my gifts or yours. What a limitation! Likely we do not rejoice enough in God's plan to give us gifts that are unique; nor do we fully appreciate the extent to which we need each other's gifts.

Is there any believer in the church to whom the Spirit has not given gifts for use in the church? Perhaps a good portion of the gifts lie dormant because they are not unearthed, developed, and encouraged. The Spirit doesn't make mistakes but determines with care the distribution of gifts. The Living Bible paraphrase of that verse says, "It is the same and only Holy Spirit who gives these gifts and powers, deciding which each one of us should have." This scripture and others call upon us to let God be God in this matter. But there are some who presume to know who can and who cannot use the gift of proclaiming God's message--with maleness often considered a qualification and femaleness a disqualification.

What are the gifts given to believers? And what is your gift and mine? We can know rather precisely what our gift is. Paul did. He said, "Christ did not send me to baptize but to preach the gospel" (I Cor. 1:17).

In I Corinthians 12, verses 8 to 10, Paul lists Spirit-given gifts: gifts of wisdom, knowledge, faith, healing, miraculous powers, prophecy, distinguishing spirits, tongues, and interpreting tongues. Consider whether your gift is in that list, or in the collection Paul notes in Romans 12:6-8: prophesying, administration, teaching, sermon delivery, encouraging, contributing to the needs of others, leadership, showing mercy.

Brothers and sisters in the faith are themselves gifts to the church. Paul says in I Cor. 12:27, "Now you are the body of Christ, and each one of you is a part of it." Then he names primarily the persons rather than the gifts: apostles, prophets, teachers, workers of miracles, healers, helpers, administrators, speakers in different languages. In Ephesians 4:11 Paul also identifies evangelists and pastors.

The Practice. Of all the gifts in these lists, which is your special gift given you by God's Spirit? I hope you will take seriously that which you know; I hope the community of believers of which you are a part will encourage and not discourage you. When we minimize our gifts, we deny the work of the Holy Spirit in our lives. Paul reminded Timothy: "Do not neglect your gift..." (I Tim. 4:14) and "Fan into flame the gift of God which is in you." (2 Tim. 1:6)

If God gives the gift of speaking or preaching, the intent is to proclaim the Divine message, not accumulate personal praises. (However,

34

finding joy in exercising gifts is appropriate.) If God gives the gift of writing, the task is to express and record God's Word of truth. If God gives the gift of singing, the opportunity is to inspire praise and edify others. If God gives the gift of caring and counseling, the responsibility is to reflect Divine care. If God gives the gift of teaching, the nurturing of searching minds should follow. Race, class, age, sex, and physical characteristics of skin, eyes, or hair will not determine whether gifts are practiced.

To encourage accountability for all gifts, perhaps congregational leaders could prepare a list of gifts and offices entitled "Your Gift(s) for the Work of the Church." Members would then be encouraged to check areas for involvement: administration, worship, nurture, education, peace and service, evangelism, prayer ministry, hospitality, financial aid. Gifts would help to determine the mission of the congregation and not be limited to filling offices. Selecting brothers and sisters for given responsibilities would be facilitated.

Small groups could discern individual's gifts through prayer and discussion. People interested and hesitant could then feel recognized and involved.

As he often does in his teaching, Paul uses the illustration of the coordinating parts of the human body to show how we need each other in the work of the church (I Cor. 12:12-21). The ear does not say, "Because I am not an eye, I do not belong to the body..." The head cannot say to the feet, "I don't need you!"

Two triple statements may help us to capture the meaning of the above passage, to keep a healthy sense of one's own and others' gifts, and to acknowledge that we all have limitations, we all are interdependent.

1. You are gifted. You are limited. I am needed.
2. I am gifted. I am limited. You are needed.

Paul says in Romans 12:6 (RSV) "Having therefore gifts that differ, let us use them." That does not foster self-apology or discouragement of another.

The Power. What is the power for the use of spiritual gifts? The Spirit not only gives the gifts; the Spirit enables their use. Paul said in I Cor. 2:4, "My message and my preaching were not with wise and persuasive words, but with a demonstration of the Spirit's power, so that your faith may not rest on human wisdom, but on God's power." Continuing in verse 13, we speak, not the manner of human wisdom but patterning the Spirit, expressing spiritual truths in spiritual words.

We have reason to believe that the Holy Spirit brings the words of Jesus to our remembrance. He had said to His disciples, "...the Counselor, the Holy Spirit, whom the Father will send in my name, will teach you all things and will remind you of everything I have said to you" (John 14:26). We can develop a new awareness and appreciation for such spirit consciousness. We might remind ourselves, however, that knowing the words of Christ first makes bringing them to our remembrance possible. Concerted study, prayer, and humbling of ourselves before God makes authentic our acts of service.

35

RUTH BRUNK STOLTZFUS

What a thrill to know that God wills a strong Spirit to dwell within us, weak and fragile as we are on our own. That enables us to serve God's purposes! Paul was conscious of this in his own life; he spoke of Christ's energy "which so powerfully works in me" (Col. 1:29).

The Purpose. What, finally, is the purpose of using our gifts? It is for the common good. "Now to each one the manifestation of the Spirit is given for the common good (I Cor. 12:7). The Living Bible paraphrases this: "The Holy Spirit displays God's power through each one of us as a means of helping the entire church." In Ephesians 4:11-13 Paul says the purpose is to prepare God's people for unity in the work of service. Referring to Jesus, who gifted some to be apostles, prophets, evangelists, pastors, and teachers, the purpose was to prepare God's people for serving "so that the body of Christ may be built up until we all reach unity in the faith and in the knowledge of the Son of God, becoming mature and attaining to the whole measure of the fullness of Christ."

Peter, that formerly unstable and impulsive disciple who became a strong man of God through the power of the Holy Spirit, speaks about the use of gifts and their purpose, "Each one should use whatever grace has been received to serve others, faithfully administering God's grace in its various forms. Whoever speaks should do it as one speaking the very words of God. Whoever helps serve should do it with the strength God provides so that in all things God may be praised through Jesus Christ..." (I Peter 4:11)

Not of ourselves or for ourselves are gifts exercised. Our purpose is not for selfish reasons but for the good of the entire church, not to impress but to help others, not to domineer but to serve others.

Self-fulfillment, though not the primary purpose, results too. Our best physical, mental, and spiritual health is realized when we develop and put to use our unique God-giftedness: whether in teaching, singing, writing, preaching or any of the myriad ways of helping. The thrill of implementing one's gift in God's work cannot be matched by any other kind of thrill. While thrilling to use one's gift, it is killing (in a sense) to be restricted from using them. But God's providential hand is over our lives, amazing us by removing all kinds of obstacles, as we permit it.

Let us determine to use our gifts in such a Spirit-led way that God will be praised, Christ will always be exalted, and others will always be blessed.

RUTH BRUNK STOLTZFUS gave versions of this message at four places in 1982: North Clinton Mennonite, Wauseon, Ohio; Bancroft Mennonite, Toledo, Ohio; Park View Mennonite, Harrisonburg, Virginia; and Grace Mennonite, Pandora, Ohio. In 1982-83 she served as interim pastor for five months at Bancroft and for one year at Grace.

Engaged
Pauline Graybill Kennel

I Peter 3:15-22
Acts 17:22-31

(This sermon was the one I preached the day I was licensed to the ministry.)

When we came home one day a couple of weeks ago, we found a note Rita had left on the kitchen table. It said, "The electricity was off for about 20 minutes this noon, so all the clocks are wrong." We all know, don't we, that electric clocks run and keep time only as long as the electric power keeps coming through the wires. They simply cannot do their work unless the power is there.

I grew up on a farm near Freeport, Illinois, and because I was the oldest child in my family, I spent quite a bit of time driving the tractor and helping my dad farm. During the busiest time in the spring I would stay home from school some days so we could get the farm work done. I learned quickly the importance of the power drive, or power take-off as some people call it. That is a heavy metal shaft which comes out the back of the tractor. The gears in the power drive can be hooked up like this to the gears of the machine the tractor pulls to do the farm work. When the gears of each are _engaged_ with the gears of the other, the power from the tractor goes through to the other piece of machinery so it can do its work--spreading, planting, mowing, shelling, or whatever that particular machine was made to do. Because the machine is _engaged_ with the tractor, it has power and is ready to do what needs to be done.

Interestingly, though, if the machine were too high off the ground--way above the alfalfa which needed to be cut to make hay--or were off to the side where it couldn't reach the wheat which needed to be harvested, it could not do its work. It not only needed the power from the tractor, it also needed to make contact with--or be _engaged_ with--the alfalfa, the

37

wheat, or whatever needed care.

Faith people through the years--those people who were used by God to change people's lives--are people who were engaged with God, the great power source. Isn't this what Paul senses in our Acts 17 reading? Paul knew God as the Creator and Parent of the entire world, but also as the very living and present God Who moved among all people--with them and for them. For Paul, the risen and living Christ was the climax of God's work. The risen Christ was reality so powerful that when Paul saw all the idols the Athenians worshipped, the Spirit within him was provoked--excited and angered, really stirred up!

Yes, Paul was surely engaged with God. But that's not all. Paul was engaged with the people around him. He noticed those idols and didn't just pass on by. He walked the streets of Athens (that fine city where brainy people gathered, many of them snobbish, often dealing only in abstract ideas). He stopped in the church (the synagogue) with all the religious leaders. He went to the marketplace, and as he stood in the Areopagus, where the Supreme Court of Athens met, he argued and preached the Word. Scripture records that Paul had prepared himself for engagement with all these people. He knew and understood the beliefs and methods of these diverse folk. He knew the philosopies and the teaching of the Epicureans and the Stoics, whom he met. He quoted their poets and writers. And so he was able to engage with them in deep discussion, stating their beliefs and sharing with them his own faith. Those who worshipped idols and unnamed gods he challenged to worship the real God. Only such a God, too alive to live in human-crafted stone or metal, is worthy of serious devotion. To the Epicureans, who believed that the gods were unconcerned with the world, he identified the living God, who relates to people as a Parent. To the Stoics, who were pantheists and believed that God is everything and everything is God, he noted God's special work in the unique One raised from the dead. Wherever he was, in the midst of the people and their work, in the midst of activity, Paul was engaged with people. Engaged with God and engaged with people.

Church people today are called to the same kind of engagement as Paul. What happens, though, if we become so busy and so preoccupied with our own affairs, that we don't take time enough for engagement with God, our power drive? The Spirit is simply not very alive in us, hardly alive enough for us to be "provoked" as was Paul. And what if we fail to be engaged with people in the midst of all of all our comings and goings? We hardly notice the people around us--in Yorktown and Oak Brook, in shopping centers, on the Chicago Northwestern train, in the office, in our classrooms, in the narthex of the church. How then can we know what they believe, how they reason, what they live for, where they hurt? Faith people like Paul show us clearly that engagement with people requires time, observation, awareness, sensitivity, caring and response. Engagement needs preparation and knowledge and commitment to really be "with" people. Because it may require some changes in our lifestyle, it is enhanced as we support each other.

People today are not that different from the people of Paul's day.
Our three big American idols--the god of materialsm, the god of power,
and the god of self--have created immense needs. These needs cry for
help, often in very camouflaged ways. I have been called to minister to
those needs. I believe that all of us in the church are called to minister in varying ways according to the gifts which have been given us. I
list six needs which I see around us.

First, there is the need for significance. "Who am I?" is the big
question for many people. Today, we may be just one in a class of 800
students in Willowbrook High School, or just one of 4,000 persons being
graduated from the University of Illinois, or just a computer number to
most of the firms with whom we do business. The tough question becomes
"Who am I?" We faith people must respond, saying in a variety of ways,
"You are a child of God." "You are special--a chosen people." "You are
so special that Jesus Christ died for you!"

Second, there is the need for meaning. "Why am I here?" Today's
generation is the first that is not really needed--to assist on the farm,
to produce in the industrial center, to teach in the school. This is the
first generation that is an economic liability rather than an asset. So
this generation struggles intensely with the need for meaning in life.
Coupled with that is our culture's obsession with materialism--the quest
for bigger, better, and greater. Material success is most important.
How can our young people win in this 1981 American culture? The number
of children, youth, and young adults who commit suicide increases at an
alarming rate. Ours is a privileged responsibility as a church to follow
Jesus in taking seriously Isaiah 40, to help people from childhood on
find meaningful partnership with God, to extend care to our world and
society.

Third, there is the need for extended family, for real closeness. We
have people, people everywhere. But people are lonely. Shallow, self-
gratifying relationships which require little time, caring, or commitment
are too often the norm. Today, 75 percent of first pregnancies begin before marriage. Families have been changing drastically. Until recently,
the typical American affluent family consisted of a father who was the
breadwinner, a mother who stayed home to nurture the family, and their
several children. Today, only 7 percent of the population of the United
States lives in a family like that. And today 10,000 young people run
away from home every week. Hear a statistic from this morning's edition
of the Sun-Times: in 1980 13,294 children ages 17 and below were filed
with the Missing Persons Section in Chicago. Thousands of runaway children are never reported because parents are too embarrassed or just don't
care. What is an appropriate response for the church? We must wake up
and be family, the family of God, for people, enabling deep sharing and
intimacy.

A fourth need today is for peacemaking skills and commitment to live
cooperatively rather than competitively. America has put her faith in
power, with a larger and larger budget for military armaments. The average family in DuPage County will contribute a Pentagon tax of $24,000

from 1981 to 1985! According to United Nations Secretary Waldheim, the world spends $1 million per minute for weaponry. But are people increasingly secure? No, they are more fearful than ever--fearful of next door neighbors and fearful of other nations. Paul would say, "O church, argue and preach and teach and live Shalom!" Be a reconciling people, as Jesus Christ was.

Fifth, there is a need for beauty, for the unique and creative. The dull routine and boredom of so many people's lives leaves them looking for that which can enhance life. But they search through drugs, cosmetics, artificial flowers, plastic decorations, and cheap entertainment. Sadly, the more that is available to our culture, the more everything is mass-produced. Correspondingly, there are fewer needs and opportunities to be creative, to enjoy simple beauty. Our task is to encourage uniqueness, creativity, and arts expression of all kinds. Let's claim for humanity our exciting birthright: created in the image of the Creator to be creative!

Sixth, the need for a sense of wonder, for losing oneself in experiences of Transcendence, surrounds us. This need relates to all the other five. (It could just as well have been listed first.) We speak so often of the "me" generation which lives for self and is frequently turned inward. To worship something greater than oneself--that God who points beyond us to things mightier and more durable than ourselves, that God who elicits devotion and relationship and partnership--is to enlarge one's vision, one's becoming, one's very being.

About ten days ago, when ordination services for 16 priests were held at St. Mary of the Lake Seminary in Mundelein (IL), two women rose with the men when the men were asked, "Are you ready to be ordained?" They answered with the men, "I am present, ready, and willing." I am happy that I don't need to participate in such a protest, for I was called to minister at Yorkfield Presbyterian Church in Elmhurst three years ago. To be licensed today is to gain additional authenticity and meaning for my ministry.

I am so happy that people have come to this occasion to represent the three groups who have played such important roles in my own pilgrimage. I am confident that my ministry is enhanced, is richer and wiser, because of all the gifts I have received from these three denominations.

1) The Mennonite Church. I was nurtured in a deeply committed Christian family in a very loving and caring fellowship at Freeport--a fellowship that called forth my gifts for music, speaking, and teaching even as a teenager. In this denomination I served as a pastor's wife for 15 years and knew considerable involvement.

2) The Church of the Brethren. I value particularly this congregation which has recommended my licensing and Bethany Theological Seminary where I received theological education. Today is a new experience with you. Other times when I participated in worship, I was at the organ or piano, directing the children's choir or singing with my family, or serving as an education consultant.

3) Yorkfield Presbyterian Church, the beautiful congregation where I

now serve. I cannot imagine a better place for me to have begun professional ministry.

I am deeply moved to be wrapped in all these warm memories connected with all three denominations. Why should my life have taken so many unexpected turns, so many varied experiences? I don't know. I only know that God has wondrously led and accompanied me all the way. I _know_ that the variety of experiences and training have equipped me in ways that I simply would not have planned. God works in marvelous ways to prepare us for ministry in Christ's name. And the Spirit is available, is with us, as we open ourselves to communication and guidance.

Join me in praising God that we are children of God. Let us praise God that we are gifted in many ways to be the church, to live as Kingdom People. Today I commit myself to even more serious engagement with God and with the people around me--on the street, in the marketplace, in the church--wherever I happen to be. As members of the Body of Christ, gifted in many wonderful ways, we have a promise that, unlike the electricity on 22nd Street, our power will not go off. But, comparable to the tractor's power drive, the job gets done only when we are engaged!

PAULINE GRAYBILL KENNEL preached this on May 24, 1981. From 1978-1982 she was Minister of Education and Nurture in the Presbyterian church referred to above. Since September 1, 1981 she is Coordinator of Chicago Area Mennonites.

The Call to Use our Gifts
Lois Barrett

Let's begin today by looking at some biblical passages--some personal stories--of how people came to use their gifts--how God and the people of God called them to use a particular gift, and how they felt about it. Let's divide into small groups and spend a few minutes reading one of the following passages and talking about these people's responses to God's calls to them.

Exodus 3:1-4:20 (Moses)
Judges 4:1-11 (Deborah and Barak)
Isaiah 6:1-8 (Isaiah)
Isaiah 49:1-7 (the Suffering Servant)
Jeremiah 1:1-10 (Jeremiah)
1 Samuel 3:1-21 (Samuel)
Luke 18:18-30 (the "rich young ruler")
Acts 9:1-22 (Ananias)

(Allow some time for brief reporting back from each small group.)

The common thread in these passages is a hesitancy to use one's gifts, to respond to God's call. We too can identify with this hesitancy. Even if we believe strongly in discerning and using gifts in the church, why is the practice often so hard?

Elizabeth O'Connor in Eighth Day of Creation writes of the fears we have about our gifts. She says, "A primary purpose of the church is to help us discover our gifts and, in the face of our fears, to hold us accountable for them so that we can enter into the joy of creating."

What are some of these fears?

One problem we have with gifts is jealousy. I Corinthians 12:14-26 speaks of the discord in the body which results when the foot wishes it were a hand, or the eye says it doesn't need the hand. Our jealous feelings are not helped by the connotation which the word "gifted" has acquired in our language. The "gifted" people are special people, we feel;

42

there are not very many of them. They are the people at the 95th or the
99th percentile. They are gifted; we are not.

That is not the language of the New Testament. 1 Corinthians 12
speaks of every member of the church having a gift. So possession of the
gift is not dependent on intelligence, age, or even spiritual maturity.
If we take that seriously, it means that there is something for every person in the church to do. It means that when we find someone for each
office on the lists which the ministry groups have compiled, we are not
done discerning gifts until something has been found for everyone.

Dietrich Bonhoeffer in Life Together says, "A community which allows
unemployed members to exist within it will perish because of them. It
will be well therefore if every member receives a definite task to perform for the community, that (s)he may know in hours of doubt that (s)he
too is not useless and unusable."

Finding a task for everyone in the church may not be easy. It entails our knowing well the needs of the congregation. We must also know
the abilities of each person whose gifts are to be discerned. And we must
be willing to create some new positions based on gifts actually available.

At Church of the Savior in Washington, D.C., each mission group of up
to nine people discerns gifts of each person in the group. Some offices
are standard among all mission groups. They are functions that any mission group needs in order to work. Someone has to be the prior, or moder-
ator, to chair meetings and to encourage using the gifts of others. Each
group has a pastor-prophet, who is to comfort and encourage as well as
challenge. Each group also has an intercessor, who prays specifically and
regularly for each member of the group. Beyond that, groups may create
new titles and functions depending on the gifts actually present and needed in the group. At a retreat conducted by Church of the Savior which I
attended a few years ago, Myra Thompson told of one mission group in which
a woman could not identify her own gift. But the group had noticed that
she was always the one who remembered birthdays or other occasions to celebrate, and who frequently organized their celebrations. That gift of
celebration was important, the group decided, and she became the group's
celebrator.

All of us need to be needed. Feeling needed is what makes us committed to a group of people and to continuing to work for the welfare of
that group. Feeling needed in a particular task helps to eliminate those
feelings of inferiority and jealousy. At Church of the Servant in Wichita
we asked new people to do particular jobs in the church right away, often
before they felt they were ready. But people grew through the experience
and they learned that there is no observer status in the church.

Jealousy can also be reduced if we are serious about eliminating implications of higher status for some duties in the church. Paul speaks
of this specifically in 1 Corinthians 12:

> On the contrary, the parts of the body which seem to be weaker
> are indispensable and those parts of the body which we think
> less honorable we invest with the greater honor, and our un-
> presentable parts are treated with greater modesty which our

LOIS BARRETT

> more presentable parts do not require. But God has so adjusted
> the body, giving the greater honor to the inferior part, that
> there may be no discord in the body, but that the members
> may have the same care for one another.

There is to be no difference in status between those who teach adults and
those who teach children, between those whose gifts require use of verbal
skills and those who are less verbal.

Not only can jealousy prevent people from using the gifts they have,
but fear of other's jealousy can inhibit the use of gifts. Those who have
been identified as "gifted" are sometimes hesitant to use their gifts because they fear others may dislike them for it. They are afraid that if
they use their gifts, they will become too "set apart," too different from
the majority. An emphasis on the equal status of all gifts can free
these people also to use their gifts in the church.

In addition to the problem of jealousy, there is often a second problem with gifts. That is lack of accountability. We often identify gifts
in a person, but then never check to see whether she is using that gift or
whether he is doing what he said he would. Or we fail to set a deadline
by which a certain task should be done. During its early years Mennonite
Church of the Servant found this surfaced with the choosing of "shepherds,"
two persons within each house church who could take primary responsibility
for pastoral care within the fellowship. The people were chosen by each
of the house churches with some care and the duties were defined. But because pastoral care was not usually a public matter, no one knew exactly
how much the shepherds were doing. Shepherds didn't even know what each
other was doing. The situation improved when the shepherds began meeting
regularly to discuss with each other what had been happening in their
roles and in the congregation.

Holding others responsible is not always a pleasant task because sometimes we must say, or we must be told, "You did not do your job well," or
"You did not do what we trusted you to do." Other times, accountability
simply means that I do my assigned task because I know that others are
counting on me, and because I care about those others who are counting on
me. I prepared my sermon for today because I knew that without my sermon,
there would be no sermon today. I felt needed.

If we are having trouble doing what we have said we would do, perhaps
our small group, or spiritual partner, or some other person can be asked
to hold us accountable. This could be done by expecting reports from us
on what we have been doing, and by their asking the right questions at the
right time.

A third hesitancy in exercising gifts in the church is fear of failure. It is natural to want not to fail. We want to appear capable to the
people around us. Deep within there is the nagging notion that if we are
not capable, we will not be loveable either. We might sing the wrong
note in public, or make the wrong decision while serving in a leadership
position, or forget what we were supposed to do.

If our project does not have the effect we wanted it to have, we are
afraid that neither others nor ourselves—or maybe even God—will think

we are worth loving. So we volunteer for nothing. This is the kind of fear that makes us identify with the saying, "It is better to be silent and be thought a fool, than to speak and remove all doubt." Fear of failure immobilizes us by telling us that our worth as persons is dependent on our performance.

Similar to the fear of failure is the fear of success. Women, especially, have often feared being successful as much as they feared failure. Society has taught us that being successful on the job or in school means being a failure in social relationships, especially with men. So some women don't pursue more schooling, while others refuse a promotion or don't apply for a job at all because they fear the failure that success might bring to them. In the church, that fear of success, combined with the normal fear of failure, has put women in a double bind. Even when leadership positions have theoretically been open to us, we have either been afraid to take the job for fear we would not do well or for fear that we would do well. The latter forces us to admit to new capabilities and responsibilities, and at the same time to risk the criticism that sometimes comes from stepping out of traditional roles for women.

There are some remedies for fear of failure. The most important of these is to allow ourselves and others room to fail. When we hold each other accountable for appropriate use of our gifts, the purpose is not so that we can say to someone who fails, "You are not a good person because you failed." The purpose is to help and encourage the person to try again or to try something different, while still affirming the worth of that person. Worth does not diminish with success or failure. We want to know that others in the church love us and that God loves us--in spite of our success or failure.

When we look at church discipline in recent decades, we may see that some people were confronted who should not have been. But the other side of our history is that too few people were confronted and brought back into fuller fellowship with the church.

The practice of confronting only a few--usually those whose offense had something to do with sex--has left the impression that all those who were not confronted are "good people." They do not need any kind of discipling. We sometimes have the notion that all those inside the church are, or should be, sinless, perfect people. The view from most of the New Testament, however, is not that those in the church have never sinned or never failed, but that those in the church have been forgiven and have set out again on the right path. Thus, to join the church is to join the band of forgiven people--pilgrims together in the direction of Christ--who are not afraid to risk because they know that, even with failure, they are still loved. Knowing that, they can risk again.

Failure can have its benefits. Failure is painful, there's no doubt about that. But the pain is bearable, and we can learn through the pain, if there are people around us who continue to love us and help us grow stronger because of the pain.

The implication of all this for gift discernment is that we need not be so afraid of our own failure or of the failure of others in the use of gifts. This does not mean we can be haphazard about discerning gifts, and it does not mean that I should agree to do a task for which I know I am not suited. But it does mean that we can claim the freedom to allow ourselves and others the opportunities to try out gifts we have only started to develop. For we know that if we fail, we have a loving community that will give us room to explore and to grow toward the light of Christ.

An assumption practiced at the Church of the Savior in Washington is that if the call you are hearing is an authentic call from God, it will come to you as "incredibly good news." If the call isn't good news to you, you don't ask others to join you in that call. You just keep searching and listening and probing yourself and the world and the Bible until you hear a call that does sound like incredibly good news. You fully expect that a call like that will come to you.

Now this doesn't mean that if your gift is to be an organist, that practicing the organ will always be fun. And if your gift is teaching, there may be days when the session just doesn't seem to be hanging together. The exercise of any gift may have tedious or unpleasant parts.

To search for and expect a gift you can use in the church may seem very person-centered. But it is also a church-centered way of identifying gifts, because any gift that an individual identifies in herself or himself has to be tested with the church to see if using that gift will be a means of building up the church.

All of us are needed for the functioning of the body of Christ. There is some particular assignment that you are called to do and another task that I am called to do. When we overcome our fears and discover our special and particular gifts, using those gifts will elicit a sense of expectancy. We will sense that our part of sharing the good news is good news to us, too.

Let us spend some time in quiet now.

Get down to your own center.

What would you most like to do in the church?

What is the gift which the Spirit has given you?

What call seems like incredibly good news?

What fears, jealousies, or other obstacles need to be overcome before you can exercise that gift?

LOIS BARRETT presented components of this sermon in two settings: Southside Fellowship, Elkhart, Indiana and Ann Arbor Mennonite Fellowship in Michigan. She completed her MDiv studies at Associated Mennonite Biblical Seminaries and will assume worship and education coordinating duties at Mennonite Church of the Servant, Wichita, Kansas.

Facing our Fears
Marilyn R. Kern

Thousands of years ago the Psalmist wrote: The Lord is my light and my salvation; whom shall I fear? The Lord is the stronghold of my life; of whom shall I be afraid?" (Psalm 27:1) That is a testimony from a person who knew what fear was—who had learned how to face it.

A system for dealing with fears is a basic element of all religions. Primitive people are surrounded by mysterious and frightening things over which they have no control. They may devise chants or rituals to feel that they <u>are</u> in control. They may at least appease the gods and keep from getting hurt.

Our children feel these forces too; they also make up comforting rituals. Just going to bed may require three bears, two dogs, a drink of water, and a night light. Others may need something more elaborate. Older children may seem to have outgrown this stage. But when they're afraid, they tend to revert to the superstitions of the ages—not stepping on cracks, or holding your breath when you run past a cemetery. Do you older folks remember how you used to manage your fears?

Now I'm not picking on smaller people. Because I have a secret about being afraid, and I wonder if you've guessed it. Did you know that inside each one of these big grownups here, there's a little scared kid? Every one of them is afraid sometimes. Some people like to go to monster movies, or read science fiction or mystery stories, or watch scary action on TV. Maybe there are some folks here who like to ride roller coasters. Why do you suppose people want to be scared? Maybe in order to test how much fear we can stand, or to prove to ourselves that we can control it. We're going to talk today about other ways of taking care of that scared kid inside all of us.

Strangely enough, some kinds of religion try to make people more afraid. In Haiti, for instance, there are authentic cases of people liter-

ally being scared to death by voodoo rites. There are instances of people
living in America right now who are so afraid of going to hell or commit-
ing the unpardonable sin, that they are living in a hell on earth. That
too is primitive religion, though it may use God-talk and quote from the
Bible. It is certainly not the kind of mature Christian faith we read
about in the second letter to Timothy: "God hath not given us the spirit
of fear; but of power, and of love, and of a sound mind." (2 Tim. 1:7)

Let's put that God-given power, and love, and sound mind to work for
us. Honestly admitting our fears is the first step toward mastering them.
Wise parents will realize their own irrational fear of storms, or dogs,
or people of other races. They will intentionally not want their contag-
ious fears to be caught by their children.

Sometimes what we fear in another is a projection of tendencies we
don't want to admit in ourselves. Take the people who "know" that if welfare money is available, nobody will try to find a job. All sorts of
statistics about how 90 percent of the people on welfare can't be employed
can be quoted. But fearful people will continue to respond emotionally--
will talk about welfare cheats--because they are afraid that if they were
given the opportunity to loaf and get paid, they might comply. And that
would be wrong! Or consider those who give lip service to "love your enemies" but who live by the belief that in the "real world" one must meet
force with force. One must do unto others before they can do unto you.
Such people endorse the arms race, because if they were in power, they
would attack those who are weaker or more vulnerable.

What sort of fears do you admit to yourself? Or to God? Do you have
a close friend with whom you can share your fears and still be accepted?
One of the great services the church can offer is to provide small group
opportunities. In that context individuals can feel freed from being on
guard lest others discover they're not the strong, brave, or good persons
they usually seem to be. Wouldn't we be fortunate if every Church School
class, from the youngest to the oldest, were a group with whom people
could honestly admit fears, from whom support and care coud be received?

If the church doesn't help us manage our fears, we may turn to other
forces in society which make promises. A lot of advertising is based on
using our fears to manipulate us. Instead of dealing with our fear of
estrangement from those we appreciate, we are alluded into thinking that
only if we use the right toothpaste or deodorant, we won't need to worry.

Fears of growing older can be eased by using Grecian Formula, or Ger-
itol, or a detergent that makes hands look younger in spite of more dishes
being washed. For the fear of failure, there are all sorts of status sym-
bols to assure a sense of success. On a more sinister level, if we're
afraid of being shot, we can easily buy a gun. That increases the chances of someone being killed. Demagogues are always ready to exploit our
fears about crime in the streets, about people who aren't like us, or about
a possible Communist conspiracy.

Now, expecting to live without fear is unreal. It is also dangerous.
One of our babies once started to crawl off a second story porch. With no
fear of what was about to happen, she could have been killed on the rocks

below. My fear--which I still sense when I remember the incident--trigger-
ed a surge of adrenalin that enabled me to act. Leaping across the porch
and grabbing her by the back of the dress in midair, I hauled her to safety
before the dress tore. If we never knew fear, we would be living in a
fool's paradise. The church should not help us avoid fear. What we need
is help in facing our fears so they do not master us.

Once upon a time, a young seminary student was desperately in need of
a job. He felt fortunate to find a nighttime job at a local restaurant.
After he finished cleaning and locking up, he could study while acting as
the night watchman. The first night on the job went well, until he settled
down with a book and all became very quiet. He began to hear strange
sounds from one direction, then another. When he got up to look, he became
aware that he was not alone. In a far corner there was a shadowy figure.
He called out, as bravely as he could, but there was no answer. All kinds
of thoughts raced through his mind. There was a door between him and the
corner--possibly he could get out if he moved quickly. On the other hand,
this was why he had been hired. And, besides, he did need the income.

A problem surfaced: he had just been told to watch, not what to do if
he found. Taking a deep breath, he remembered his mother's advice: "Always
go toward something you're afraid of." No other wisdom came immediately to
mind, so he began walking toward the shape. Sure enough, as he did, a man
came toward <u>him</u>, silently, menacingly....Then he discovered the mirror!

Go toward the thing you fear. That's good advice. Be very specific
about what you fear. When you do, it might no longer be a threat. Or, if
it is, you've at least cut it down to a manageable size.

Many people live in a kind of nameless dread, or general anxiety, that
saps their strength while impeding progress. Some people are afraid to see
a doctor for fear cancer will be found. So they worry, instead of checking
out the basis for their worry. Fear of unemployment may not have so much
to do with loss of income as with conviction that personal worth is measured in a job. Hysteria over the threat of a Communist takeover may narrow
down to a specific fear that godless Communism is stronger than God. Focusing such factors combines the rational with the emotional.

When we specifically assess our fears, we find that some can be handled through preventive measures. If we're afraid to face a certain teacher
unprepared, we can use that fear as an extra motivation to be ready for
that class. If part of our dread of growing old is a fear of being useless
after retirement, we can begin long before that time to develop interests
which will continue to give life meaning, whether employed or not. If we
are afraid of losing a job, we can start preparing for something else we'd
really like to do. If we have fear of tornadoes, we can build a storm
cellar, or develop an emergency plan with the family, so everyone knows
what to do when we hear the warning. If we think we have detected one of
the warning signals of cancer, we can go to the doctor immediately to find
out. If it isn't cancer, we can stop worrying. If it is, our prompt action may make cure more possible.

But what if it can't be cured? Not all disasters can be prevented.
We need to face this fact honestly and vigorously. What if the thing you

fear most comes to pass? What is the worst thing that can happen? You
can face it.

Don't most of our fears cluster around the thought of death? You know
Jesus faced death more than once. Once people were so angry with one of
his sermons that, according to Luke, "They led him to the brow of the hill
on which their city was built, that they might throw him down headlong."
Luke continues: "But passing through the midst of them, he went away."
(Luke 4:30) What happened? That primitive kid in us may want to believe
that Jesus used his magic powers to escape. But I think the answer is more
profound than that, and more useful to those of us who don't have such powers. In a later chapter, Luke quotes Jesus: "I tell you, my friends, do
not fear those who kill the body, and after that have no more that they
can do." (Luke 12:4)

Jesus lived his whole life that way, and we can too. I think this is
what gave Paul the courage to face beatings, shipwreck, and one threat on
his life after another. What was the worst that could happen to him?
He writes to the Romans, and to us, "If we live, we live to the Lord, and
if we die, we die to the Lord; so then, whether we live or whether we die,
we are the Lord's." (Romans 14:8)

Have you ever tried to tell a child who's afraid of the dark "Stop
crying! There's nothing to be afraid of!" Did it work? If instead you
put your arms around that little one, offering closeness rather than commands, you could probably feel the tension start to leave the little body.
When we face our worst fears, when we are driven to the limits of what
we can endure, we discover truth that has sustained people through the ages:
"The eternal God is your dwelling place, and underneath are the everlasting arms." (Deuteronomy 33:27)

Have you been recalling fearful people you know? Are they pretty
wrapped up in themselves? Self-centeredness breeds fears; being concerned
about others helps us to live above our fears, as Jesus did. 1 John 4:18
suggests: "There is no fear in love, but perfect love casts out fear."
Turning our attention to the needs of others assists us in being more
fearless.

Some time ago I read a true story in Fellowship magazine ("Safe Passage," by Dorothy T. Samuel, April 1975) of two young women in Philadelphia
who went out one night to pay their rent. They were returning home along
an empty street, literally empty-handed, when a man with a knife jumped out
at them and demanded money. One could have gotten away, but instinctively
they each knew that that would mean the sacrifice of the other. Nervously
the man said:

"I don't want to do this. I don't like to hurt people. But
sometimes I have to."
"But you can see--we don't have any money."
"I have to have money!"

They began to realize that he was irrational--maybe badly in need of
a fix. He really didn't want to do this--perhaps he was even more frightened than they. But now he couldn't let them go for fear of their calling
the police.

"Look, come back with us. I have some money in my apartment."

"It's a trick. You'll call the police."

"Trust us. We'll get you the money."

He began to move with them as they talked to him calmly. When they reached the apartment, one woman took her place under the knife while the other went in. All she could find was a ten dollar bill. She ran back to the hallway to give it to him.

"Is that all you have?"

"That's all; that's really all!"

"But I only need $5. I don't have change."

From threat to apology! The role of stick up man had been lost when the young women refused the role of terrified victims.

"That's all right. You take it. 'Bye now."

With that, he left. They could then collapse and realize how frightened they had been. But they were elated too, and still concerned about him. He was so miserable, so scared. Scared of being caught. Scared of people who refused to meet him with responses he understood. When a man has geared himself to hate and threaten and even murder, what can he say in the face of a simple, human response? What can he do with two young women who say "Trust us"?

Now, maybe you would quarrel with the way they handled it--and you could be right. Not every story like that would have such a happy ending. But at least it exemplifies the advice to Timothy, "God hath not given us the spirit of fear; but of power, and of love, and of a sound mind." The author of the article suggests:

> As long as we have a society in which existence for some is so
> miserable that they would rather blank out than adjust, these
> confrontations will occur. But we can prepare ourselves to
> face these situations. We can armor ourselves inside, prepare
> an impregnable identity which does not grovel before threat,
> nor lose all initiative in human encounter. We can carry our
> own world and our own values within us, project them around us.
> We can greatly increase our chances of dominating any encounter
> with the frustrated and the alienated and the confused who have
> no weapon against society but violence and threat and brutal-
> ity. We may not always succeed--there is no magic formula by
> which every human being can always prevail against any of the
> dangers of existence.

But rather than allowing our lives to be dominated by fear of those who murder and rape, we can imagine creative responses to the worst that could happen. Then we have a bank of positive, carefully considered, Christian options for our reflexes to choose from if we encounter an emergency. Like the seminary student who carried with him his mother's advice, we can be developing now the inner resources which will sustain us in our times of testing.

How can we face our fears?

Honestly admit what we fear.

Go toward that which we fear.

MARILYN R. KERN

    Be concerned about the needs of others.
    Anticipate, even the worst, knowing that God is with us.
For "Who shall separate us from the love of Christ? Shall tribulation, or
distress, or persecution, or famine, or nakedness, or peril, or sword?...
No, in all these things we are more than conquerors" through the One who
loves us. (Romans 8:35, 37)
    Thanks be to God!

MARILYN R. KERN preached this sermon at First Mennonite Church, Bluffton,
Ohio where she was former Assistant Pastor. She is currently completing
her Ph.D. dissertation in the field of Biblical Interpretation.

John Donne's Sins
Sara Kreider Hartzler

(SARA KREIDER HARTZLER was an English professor at Goshen College, a copy
editor for <u>Mennonite Quarterly Review</u>, and mother of three young daughters
when she died of cancer November 8, 1982, at the age of 39. A portion of
this sermon was read at her funeral.)

It's one of the oldest, the simplest, and the most profound truths of
Christianity that Christians, saved Christians, still sin. This situation
is the cause of great frustration and great spiritual anguish even among
those who devote their entire lives, their entire energies, to the service
of the Lord. It's almost shocking to hear the degree of frustration, the
intensity of the anguish in St. Paul's famous statement about his struggle
with sin, in Romans 7:14-24. Let's look at it again together:

> The law is spiritual, but I am not. I am unspiritual, the
> purchased slave of sin....For what I do is not what I want to
> do, but what I detest....The will to do good is there; the deed
> is not. The good which I want to do I fail to do, but what I
> do is the wrong which is against my will....In my inmost self
> I delight in the law of God, but I perceive there is in my
> bodily members a different law, fighting against the law that
> my reason approves and making me a prisoner....Miserable crea-
> ture that I am, who is there to rescue me? (NEB)

These are the words of Paul, of all people, one of the greatest and surely
one of the most self-assured leaders that the Church has ever known.

What makes the situation so intense is the paradox that the more Christian a person is--that is, the more aware one is of the overwhelming greatness and perfection of God--the more dreadful one's personal sins seem to
be. Here's the way it works: Christianity, as we all know, is a revealed
religion. We are inspired by the Holy Spirit. We receive revelation. We
accept salvation. And when we pray, we don't pray to our ancestors or to

our own vital forces, variously defined; we are praying to God.

What all that means is that the source of Christianity is not inside ourselves. It is outside ourselves, because the source of Christianity is God. So if God Himself is the source, God is also the standard, the focus, the object of our belief, and of all our hope.

Now this fact means that the Christian is under the obligation constantly to measure all his thoughts, all his actions, and all his feelings against what he knows God wants him to be. That is, the Christian has to conduct his life, he has to think all of his thoughts, he has to feel all of his feelings, in the presence of God. So it really isn't enough for a Christian to crow "O praise the Lord" or to hug himself and say "I feel so good about God." No. The Christian has to function within the constant awareness of who God is, who God wants him as a human to be, and what God wants him to do about that.

Now Paul was one of those lucky Christians who was able to agonize over his sinful inclinations in the presence of God and yet very confidently dismiss the whole issue. The end of the Romans 7 passage is a thundering hallelujah on the organ with all stops out: "Who is there to rescue me (from my sin)? God alone, through Jesus Christ our Lord! Thanks be to God!"

Well, Paul's confidence may inspire us, but Paul's faith can only save Paul. The rest of us, sinful as we are, must each one stand in the presence of the almighty God, and work out our salvation somehow on our own, one by one.

One of the great benefits that I've gotten from study of English literature is that in literature we can find over and over again the testimonies of extremely articulate Christians who had the faith and the courage to evaluate their condition humbly and prayerfully in the presence of God. These people are not for the most part saints and patriarchs of the church. They are not Paul. They are ordinary men and women who lived in historical situations that I can understand because they're close to my own. But they were dedicated Christians who took the time to work through their deepest religious confrontations on paper, and then they lavished the love and the care on that subject to make it very beautiful and very satisfying to read.

One of the finest of these statements, these records of the confrontation between the sinner and his God, is "A Hymn to God the Father." The man who wrote it, John Donne, was a very interesting person. He lived in England during the Reformation, a time when the whole English countryside was seriously reconsidering what it believed about God. Now by the time he was thirty-five years old, John Donne had a Doctorate of Divinity from Cambridge. He was an ordained Anglican minister, was dean of a large London church, and taught theology in a private college.

But the man wasn't all piety. He courted his wife in some of the most sensitive and seductive love poetry in the English language, and then he eloped with her when he was about thirty and she was not quite sixteen. His enthusiasm for his good wife continued; they had twelve children over the next sixteen years. So John Donne was a very human kind of person, a serious, sexy, wholly passionate man with a very good sense of humor, whose children's love and respect for him extended long after his death. In short, he was the kind of person that most of us would like to be.

Now let's see what this kind of man had to say in the presence of God:

A Hymn to God the Father

Wilt Thou forgive that sin where I begun,
    Which is my sin, though it were done before?
Wilt Thou forgive that sin through which I run,
    And do run still, though still I do deplore?
        When Thou hast done, Thou hast not done,
            For I have more.

Wilt Thou forgive that sin which I have won
    Others to sin? and made my sin their door?
Wilt Thou forgive that sin which I did shun
    A year or two, but wallowed in a score?
        When Thou hast done, Thou hast not done,
            For I have more.

I have a sin of fear, that when I have spun
    My last thread, I shall perish on the shore;
Swear by Thy self, that at my death Thy Son
    Shall shine as he shines now and heretofore;
        And, having done that, Thou hast done,
            I fear no more.

Like every good poem, this one has a beginning, a middle section that moves to a climax, and an end. The situation, the beginning point here, is exactly the same one that we sang in Hymn 233: "Depth of mercy! Can there be/ Mercy still reserved for me?" John Donne is confessing his sins, and he's seeking God's forgiveness. Donne knows that he isn't really worthy of mercy. So he humbly asks for forgiveness in a series of questions. We expect him to begin with the smallest sin, and as he gathers courage and gets into the swing of things, he'll work up to the greatest one--that is, sort of saving the worst for last. But right away in this poem John Donne gives us a surprise: "Wilt Thou forgive the sin where I begun,/ Which is my sin, though it were done before?" The sin he's referring to is original sin, the sin of Adam and Eve, the big one which made salvation necessary for human beings.

But almost like a Mennonite, Donne brushes aside the original sin for mere openers. His second class of sins, however, are those which are quite clearly his own fault: "Wilt Thou forgive those sins through which I run,/ And do run still, though still I do deplore?" These are the sins that he's known all along were dead wrong, but he can't seem to stop doing them. Now you don't get the particulars. You can fill in your own bad habits-- overeating, gossip, bad tempers, screaming at the kids--fill in the blanks. But Donne wraps up this first unit of the confession with the refrain, "When Thou hast done, thou hast not done,/ For I have more." That is, when you've done what I've asked you, Lord, and forgiven me, you still aren't finished, because I have a lot more to confess.

Now verse two pushes on to very much more serious matters: "Wilt Thou forgive that sin (by) which I have won/ Others to sin? and made my sin their door?" To cause your brother to sin blackens not only your own soul but his too, and that's a pretty terrible responsibility, particularly for a clergyman like John Donne, whose business in life is to lead his congregation toward God, not away from God.

But John Donne knows that there are sins that are a lot worse than being a bad example: "Wilt Thou forgive that sin which I did shun/ A year or two, but wallowed in a score?" Here Donne refers to what used to be called in my grandfather's church backsliding. To revert to a sin that you once had the guts to overcome and to allow yourself to continue in that lapse is a greater sin than the original wrongdoing was, because both you and God know that you _can_ do better; you just _aren't_. And there seems to be very little excuse for that.

But verse three is where Donne and the poem finally get to the heart of things. This is the big one; this is the one that he's been working himself up to confess: "I have a sin of fear, that when I have spun/ My last thread I shall perish on the shore." He's saying that when he has woven the last thread of action into the fabric of his life, when he comes to the banks of River Jordan, he's afraid he isn't going to make it across into the Promised Land. Or, to say it another way, he's afraid that death really will be the end, not only of life but of everything. He's afraid that maybe there is no afterlife, that when he dies there will be nothing, and he will perish--that's his word, "perish"--absolutely and forever.

Recently, as I'm sure you are aware, there have been a lot of studies on death and dying, and they come to various conclusions. But there's one point on which all these studies agree. All of us, all human beings, are afraid to die. This fear is so universal that anybody who claims never to have experienced it is either extremely young, a total liar, or mentally deficient. In fact, the fear of death seems to be absolutely normal and absolutely natural. We seem to be made that way, and so people like Kubler-Ross and others tell us that since the fear of death is so universal and so normal, it's okay, and we really shouldn't feel bad about it at all.

And yet, from the language Donne is using and the position he is giving the point in the structure of his poem, John Donne very clearly believes that this normal, this universal fear is the greatest and worst sin that he can and does commit against his God. Why? All the other sins on Donne's list are sins either of omission or commission, things that one does or things that one neglects to do. All, that is, except the first one, original sin. We're told very clearly in the Bible that all of us have sinned and come short of the glory of God, and that all of us, however morally we live, need salvation. Jesus, of course, made salvation possible, so original sin to a believing Christian isn't much of a threat.

But there is one hitch: if we are all sinners, even forgiven sinners, what is "normal" or "natural" or even "universal" in the human condition is not God-like. God, after all, calls us to become a new creation. And we

56

become that new creation by an act of faith. We believe that Jesus is the means to our salvation. We believe that the tomb was empty on Easter morning, and that Jesus literally and factually rose from the dead. This is the real core, after all, of Christianity. Most of the rest of what we profess is either morals or ethics, and the Christian humanists are quick to swipe it. But this one thing is faith, and it's absolutely central.

When we remember, then, what faith is, I think it becomes clear why the fear of death is really the greatest sin of all. It is the sin against faith. The fear of death is doubting Jesus. It's doubting salvation, and worst of all, it is doubting not only the promises, but the very existence of God. It is a terrible sin. It is a horrible sin, but we all have it anyway.

John Donne was an honest man, and he admitted his fear without excuse and without evasion. But Donne was also a Christian man and a holy man, and his solution to his dilemma is still the very best one that we have. Faced with what is the ultimate sin, he turns to God for strength and reassurance: "Swear by Thy self, that at my death Thy Son/ Shall shine as he shines now and heretofore." He is saying two things at once in these two lines, and both of them are very important. When he asks God to "Swear by Thy self," he is asking for reassurance that is based on the only fixed, sure, and unchangeable things in this universe and beyond--God.

And notice what he is asking God to reaffirm. In different printings of this poem, the word "Son" is also spelled "Sun." What Donne is asking is that the very physical order that God has created--the sun and the moon and the seasons and the cycles of life--is going to continue, is going to remain stable, is going to remain predictable, that natural law as God ordained it will go on. But Donne is also asking that the spiritual order which God has ordained will continue. He's asking that God's son Jesus will shine as strongly and as dependably in his spiritual life as the physical sun shines on the earth. And that he, John Donne, will see the light of Christ as clearly at his death as he did at the time of his conversion. Again in the old Biblical phrase, Donne is saying, "Lord, I believe; help Thou my unbelief."

And then we come to the refrain. This time it's slightly different: "And having done that, Thou hast done"--not only Thou hast "finished," but also Thou hast "Donne"--John Donne. You have John Donne as a soul devoted to and now belonging entirely to his God. And Donne concludes, "I have no more"--nothing more to confess, no more doubt, no more fear. It isn't exactly St. Paul's "God alone has rescued me through Jesus Christ our Lord; thanks be to God!" But then John Donne, like most of the rest of us, isn't St. Paul. Yet John Donne prayerfully and with God's support has passed the last and the very hardest test of the Christian faith. He is now able to die.

SARA KREIDER HARTZLER preached this sermon at Eighth St. Mennonite Church, Goshen, IN, July 30, 1978, and at Prairie St. Mennonite Church, Elkhart, IN, November 16, 1980.

"Go Tell it on the Mountain"
Diane L. MacDonald

(In this sermon Diane offers a tribute to Sara Kreider Hartzler. Information about Sara's death appears at the beginning of her sermon, p. 53. This reflects further on her life.)

One of the benefits of visiting relatives on holidays is exposure to new literature. This Christmas among the usual magazines and travel books on the coffee table lay a new paperback, <u>Real Men Don't Eat Quiche</u>. The book begins with a truck driver bemoaning the loss of real men in America today and eventually gets around to that all-American pastime of dumping on Alexander Haig. Now the reason Mr. Haig does not qualify as a real man is the type of answers he was known for giving the press during his sojourn in the present administration. Here's a sample:[1]

Question: Mr. Haig, is this administration going to increase or decrease the federal budget?

Mr. Haig: Well, according to our latest reports, at this point in time, within the usual parameters, allowing for the normal fluctuations, and unpredictable variables--and subject to a reassessment in a different timeframe--answer-wise, I'd have to respond to your query with a definite guarded affirmative: based on present information, the odds are good that the federal deficit will either go up or down.

I won't offend you by repeating the author's one-word assessment of this answer. Whether deserved or not, Mr. Haig failed the test. When clarity and conviction were demanded, only a polished hedging was offered, and the people deserved more.

This critique of Mr. Haig comes closer to home for us liberal Christians when the subject matter changes from politics to faith. We do not lack clarity and conviction in our pleas for a just and peaceable world. For example, we can take pride in the leadership our churches have taken in condemning the stocking of nuclear arsenals and cold war tactics. In many cases, we are in the forefront of society denouncing this and other threats to the well-being of humanity. And this is good.

But this clear voice of proclamation does break down at times—and often with the crucial area of the meaning of faith. We have little trouble cursing the death wrought by weapons and war. What do we say to a friend dying of cancer of the meaning of life and of everlasting life? We have little trouble extolling the power of relationship, of community, of the network of love in the global community. And this is good and important. Yet how does that fit with the love of God? And the nature of prayer? What is miracle? And what of that intangible transcendance within our lives and our churches called the Spirit of God?

We don't want the simplistic, dogmatic answers to faith offered on our TV screens. And we don't need a bumpersticker gospel. For many of us, those answers have been at best irrelevant and at worst destructive. Yet, in a world where death reigns in different degrees in so many hearts and lives, that clear word of testimony is demanded and deserved.

I was reminded of this challenge for myself last November through my friend Sara. Sara taught with me at Goshen College. She had gotten her doctorate in English Literature and then married, had three children, and was teaching part time. Her office was next to mine, so we would commiserate about juggling family and profession. We also had good provocative talks—not the least of which was arguing about theology.

In her classes Sara was a terror to first-year writing students. Not only was she a stickler about grammar and spelling, she had determined that the only really unforgivable sin was word inflation. So most papers returned to students their first semester with Sara were bleeding with red ink. The writing improved remarkably that term as did student appraisal of their professor.

This past October Sara was told she had cancer with six months to live. A mutual friend wrote me and said that Sara wanted a letter from me. I struggled with that for over a week. It was a busy time of the term for me so I got up at 3 a.m. for several days and tried to write. The letter had to be concise, clear, and nothing less than the most honest and deeply held word of hope that my faith could proclaim. I was still struggling when I got a call on a Monday in early November that Sara might die that night. She survived the night. I left a message by phone. I also wrote Sara. A few days later, she died. In life, Sara had given me the gifts of her talent and spirit. In death, she gave me the gift of demanding a declaration of my faith.

Go Tell It on the Mountain is a proclamation of Christian faith best known through song. It is also the title of a 1950's novel by James Baldwin on the conversion and proclamation of a black preacher, Gabriel. The song resounds with a simple proclamation of faith: Go Tell It on the Mountain that Jesus Christ is Born. This is the stuff of Baldwin's own upbringing, his own pilgrimage as a teenage preacher in Harlem. It's his own cross to bear and possibly also his own path of salvation.

One way Baldwin struggles with this proclamation of Jesus is by contrasting the conversion experience of the preacher Gabriel with his stepson, John. Gabriel had been bad--mean, carousing, a low-down, spoiled and selfish guy. Then he met the Lord. He met the Lord on a mountaintop--one that he Gabriel had climbed. And standing up there looking down at that steep hard slope that he had conquered, Gabriel stood tall and straight before God and received the promise that he and his seed should be the elect.

What Gabriel proclaimed thereafter through word and deed was powerful, applauded by the congregation, and acknowledged as God's own word--by all, that is, except those who knew him best. His life as God's annointed had left a trail of human destruction behind him. His first wife, his mistress, his son, his sister, his second wife, his stepson and his second son all felt the terrible destruction of his pride and judgement, and they hated him. As captured in his sister's perceptive plea: "Who is you met Gabriel, all your holy life long, you ain't made to drink a cup of sorrow? And you doing it still--you going to be doing it till the Lord puts you in your grave."[2]

One night Gabriel's stepson John who wanted nothing to do with his father's gospel was grabbed by God in a fit of penitence right on the floor of their storefront sanctuary. And this was no mountaintop. As Baldwin describes it:[3]

> ...something moved in John's body which was not John. He was
> invaded, set at naught, possessed. This power had struck John,
> in the head or in the heart; and, in a moment, wholly filling
> him with an anguish that he could not endure, that even now he
> could not believe, had opened him up; had cracked him open, as
> wood beneath the axe cracks down the middle, as rocks break up;
> had ripped him and felled him in a moment, so that John had not
> felt the wound, but only the agony, had not felt the fall, but
> only the fear; and lay here, now, helpless, screaming, at the
> very bottom of darkness.

Now that's not a typical stage of faith development that we are accustomed to endorsing here at Iliff. Yet for Baldwin there is a note of authenticity and hope in this conversion that wasn't in Gabriel's. When John had suffered the deep agony of that lonesome valley, he was lifted up. He did not climb. He could not climb. He was lifted up from that darkness into light. He wanted to shout and he wanted to cry out. He wanted to find his mother and to comfort her, but "the night had given him no language, no second sight, no power to see into the heart of any other. He knew only...that the heart was a fearful place."[4]

Baldwin ends the novel right there, so we really don't know what John proclaimed thereafter. That Jesus would indeed be proclaimed, we know, and that the proclamation would differ radically from that of his father's we also know. John's real struggle had only begun, but so had his joy and his salvation.

There is great risk in proclamation. As confirmed by Baldwin, two people in the same religious tradition speaking similar words of faith can both voice a proclamation of word and deed. One can condemn and one redeem. One results in a curse and the other in a blessing. One leads to death and the other leads to life. Proclamation is clarity of thought and power of expression. It promotes change. And that change has as much power for destruction as for renewal of life and soul. To proclaim that "Jesus saves" is not neutral. Perhaps in this context, we do well to remember that it is also not necessarily an unthinking, dogmatic reflection of a religiously conservative paranoia. Given an appropriate context, "Jesus saves" can be a courageous proclamation of authentic faith that is liberating and humane.

Politicians know the risk of clearly stated convictions. Their adeptness at smokescreens and diversionary tactics is often what keeps them in office. But as people of faith we don't have that luxury. It's not just that we're in church leadership or training to be there: the demand is much more profound than that. The demand is in the nature of life itself as we know it. The demand is in the cry of all humankind in our differing forms of poverty of life and spirit. Just as I felt the demand for a declaration of faith from a dying friend, so we all should hear the demand in all the kinds of death gripping the bodies and souls of the human community. We are all called to speak a word of hope, a word that is authentic, loving, and as persuasive as the threat of death itself.

The words that we are called to proclaim won't all sound the same. God's grace has many faces and voices. But one voice most of us can hear is that of the gospel spiritual. Fannie Lou Hammer--theologian, preacher, activist for Civil Rights, and caretaker of people in the churches, fields, highways, and prisons of the Mississippi Delta--was known to sing with gusto the song, "Go Tell It on the Mountain." But she changed the words somewhat. Along with proclaiming that Jesus Christ was born, she sang:

Go tell it on the mountain, over the hills, and everywhere.

Go tell it on the mountain, to let my people go.
Her life of tough love gave those proclamations of Jesus and liberation their authenticity and truth.[5]

On this day when we celebrate the light of faith shining forth in the darkness, I urge you to explore the gospel. Struggle with its meaning in the whole context of your study and life. Discover your own words of hope, and then risk proclaiming them far and near. If authentic and molded by God's Spirit, the proclamation will echo throughout the hearts and minds of others and return to you with gifts of peace.

[1]This is an altered form of an answer by Alexander Haig in Real Men Don't Eat Quiche by Bruce Feirstein, (New York: Pocket Books, 1982), p. 29.

[2]James Baldwin, Go Tell It On The Mountain, (New York: Dell Publishing, 1953), p. 212.

[3]Ibid., p. 193.

[4]Ibid., pp. 206-207.

[5]Edwin King, "Go Tell It On The Mountain," Sojourners, (Dec. 1982),p. 18.

DIANE L. MACDONALD gave this chapel presentation on the Day of Epiphany, January 6, 1983 at the Iliff School of Theology, Denver, Colorado. She is a campus minister with the ecumenical organization located on the University of Denver campus in Colorado.

Waiting for God: Waiting in Darkness
Marlene Kropf

(Editor's note: The following are <u>excerpts</u> from an Advent Vesper series
planned by a group of women for their congregation.)

> From the beginning till now the entire creation, as we
> know, has been groaning in one great act of giving
> birth; and not only creation, but all of us who possess
> the first fruits of the Spirit, we too groan inwardly
> as we wait for our bodies to be set free. Romans 8:22, 23

We wait patiently, and we wait in darkness.

This is the dark time of the year. Soon the shortest day will come.
It will be a day in which we see dim light for only a few brief hours.

In THE IRRATIONAL SEASON, Madeleine L'Engle tells of going with her
children to a planetarium to hear a lecture. There they learned that

> ...primitive people used to watch the sun drop lower on the
> horizon in great terror, because they were afraid that one
> day it was going to go so low that it would never rise again;
> they would be left in unremitting night. There would be weep-
> ing and wailing and gnashing of teeth, and a terror of great
> darkness would fall upon them. And then, just as it seemed that
> there would never be another dawn, the sun would start to come
> back; each day it would rise higher, set later.[1]

In the Christian church, Advent is the beginning of the church year.
It is a dark beginning. Just like the ancient Israelites who spent 400
years between the Old and New Testaments submerged in darkness, with no
word from God, we too wait these four weeks in the darkest time of the
year.

We wait for God....

Several weeks ago I heard of a woman whose severe heart pains neces-
sitated her being in a doctor's office on the afternoon of Christmas Eve.

After some testing, her doctor asked her what she had been doing for the past month. When she completed the lengthy list of sewing projects, cooking and baking, choir rehearsals, and the seven parties she had given, he told her quite frankly that all she needed was a vacation, not medication....In her despair she realized the truth about her heart pains. All her frantic efforts to prepare for Christmas had not prepared her for God's coming at all. She had thrown aside centuries of Christian wisdom which marked Advent as a time of waiting for the glorious day of birth.

...

I remember what Advent was like for me last year. I wrote in my journal:

Throughout this Christmas season my thoughts of you, my God, have been blurred, distorted, dimmed by an overlay of suffering. I keep seeing the suffering Polish people whom I love; I see my own flesh and blood brother in his hopelessness in the alcoholics' rehabilitation center; I feel frightened in my home because one of my sisters in the congregation was raped last week....Where are you, my God, in the midst of human suffering?

...

And so we simply accept the marvelous mystery: we come before God, just as we are. And we are freely given new life.

The Psalmist says, "The darkness is not dark to thee. The night is bright as the day for darkness is as light with thee." (Ps. 139:12) In this darkness, which is light with thee, we wait for God.

But sometimes for personal reasons, God hides from us. Frederick Buechner says:

> Just as sacramental theology speaks of a doctrine of the Real Presence, maybe it should speak also of a doctrine of the Real Absence because absence can be sacramental too, a door left open, a chamber of the heart kept ready and waiting.[2]

What is keeping the chambers of our hearts ready and waiting for God like?

Simone Weil, in WAITING FOR GOD, says that waiting for God is paying attention to God. Paying attention, really paying attention, is not an easy thing to do. We are so full of ourselves that really paying attention to another is hard. Have you ever caught yourself formulating an answer to someone's question before the person has even finished asking the question?

When we pay attention to God, we hold back our own preconceptions and our desires for how things should be until God has had a chance to make an impact on us. This kind of attention is closely related to repentance, for we allow God to move us and change us. And when that happens, we are full of gratitude and joy. Attention to God also purifies our attention to the world and provides the energy and light we need in order to be in the world.

I think this kind of waiting for God, this paying close attention, is something like a woman waiting to give birth.

I remember two distinctly different experiences when I waited to give

birth to our children. My husband and I lost our first child when I was
about five months pregnant. I remember lying in the hospital, waiting
in labor for four days, and all that time fighting and fighting against
that birth....

The child was born and died, and I was filled with despair. I came
home from the hospital and alone, on Easter morning, I wept while much
of Christendom celebrated the resurrection of our Lord.

Sometimes our waiting for God is like that. We hold out our arms,
and they remain empty. God seems very far away. But there is another
kind of waiting....A year later I was in the hospital again. This time
I was roundly pregnant with a full-term baby. And what a difference!

As the labor pains came stronger and stronger, I found myself saying,
"Come on, little one! You can make it! Come on!" I was the cheering
section. Instead of fighting and holding back, I was exerting all my
energy toward birth. And before long, there was our baby, shrieking and
squalling.

In the rhythm of life, there is darkness before there is light.
There is waiting before fulfillment. There is the question before the
answer.

And so in Advent we are waiting for a birth. We are waiting for
God. In the darkness. While leaving open the chambers of of our hearts.

---

[1]Madeleine L'Engle, <u>The Irrational Season</u>, (New York: Seabury Press,
1977), p. 2.

[2]Frederick Buechner, <u>Telling the Truth</u>, (San Francisco: Harper and
Row, 1977), p. 43.

MARLENE KROPF included these excerpts in her sermon during the Advent
series at her congregation, Portland Mennonite, Portland, Oregon, in
November 1982.

He was Broken
Elsie Miller

Luke 22:19; Mark 14:22; Matthew 26:26

They were eating--they were having a fellowship meal. They were communing with the Holy One and they were communing with each other.

Our most basic need, what we really want, according to Ruel Howe, is "to be at one with someone, to have someone who can be at one with us, and through whom we can find at-oneness with all."

Communion means "Koinonia" or fellowship. It's called "Holy" because Christians believe they are communing with the Holy One--Christ is present. At Holy Communion we catch a glimpse of the almost unbearable preciousness and mystery of life. Something holy happens.

You are not alone here partaking of communion. It is not only between Thee and me, but includes we who are a body. We who are sisters and brothers. We share in communion; we celebrate together. Anabaptists said, "None is to receive it alone." When we stress the meaning of communion, we also stress relationships.

T   How does this communion service help us relate to God? Is this a time
H   of confession, repentance, forgiveness, joy--a time of celebration?
E   Is there an emptying and an infilling? What is being emptied out?
E   Does participation in the suffering and death of Jesus bring you close
    to the suffering heart of God? Do your own hurts take on a cosmic sig-
    nificance as they are lifted into the pain of God? Do you feel more
    in tune with God? Lifted into the stream of Divine, on-going purpose?
    Committed to Kingdom building?

W   What sense of oneness do you feel with others who are communing? What
E   sense of oneness do you feel as you realize anew that you are a member
    of the Body of Christ? What sense of oneness do you feel with the
    Church of the centuries?

M   Does this service--partaking of the elements--improve your self image?
E   Is there a new sense of identity--of the indwelling Christ? Are you
     more dedicated to doing God's will? Is there new hope for the final
     outcome--in the ultimate meaning of life? What is your experience as
     you approach the table, as you await receiving the elements, as you
     leave?
     I remind you of several sources. A writing in Sanskrit says:
        Walk together, talk together,
        O ye people of the earth;
        Then and only then shall ye have peace."
And a quotation from "The Merchant of Venice" states:
        I will buy with you, sell with you, talk with you, walk with you
        and so following...but...
        I will not eat with you, drink with you, nor pray with you."
A litany entitled: "Ritual of Communion" suggests:
        Together
              walk together, eat together, drink together.
        Then we can
              talk together, work together, celebrate together,
              play together, be together.
     Observing communion can have relational, social, and political impli-
cations. As the Twelve were eating, dining, fellowshipping, Jesus took a
common food and did an uncommon thing. The act had far-reaching consequences. He used bread as an object lesson
        He took bread. Blessed it. Broke it.
        He gave it to them, and said,
        "Take, eat; this is my body."
--Did anyone attending that meal realize the importance of this statement,
  this moment?
--Was anyone aware that the course of history was about to be altered
  irrevocably?
--This launching of a communal meal would be celebrated by millions upon
  millions of followers--in almost every country, using diverse languages,
  now having been observed on the moon.
--Did people sense that they were in the presence of the world's greatest
  human being? One who would inspire more music, books, and poetry than
  any person in history?
--The living Christ met them at that fellowship meal; as we keep remembering, Christ meets us too. "Do this in remembrance of me."
--That night in the Upper Room, I suspect Jesus baffled those gathered
  friends by using simple, common, ordinary, everyday materials to teach
  them a most important lesson.
        Jesus took bread--simple bread, ordinary bread--
        and said, "This is my body."
This implies, "I am always with you. Wherever you are, I am there. My
life is forever yours, broken, poured out, given to you." That was a
pledge of unbreakable friendship.
     Now while we do not live by bread alone, neither do we live long

without it. To eat bread is to acknowledge our dependence, both on food and on each other. Frederick Buechner explains,

"To eat this particular meal together is to meet at the level of our most basic humanness, which involves our need not just for food, but for each other.

I need you to help fill my emptiness just as you need me to help fill yours. As for the emptiness that's still left over, well, we're in it together. Maybe it's most of what makes us human and makes us brothers."

Another quote suggests,

"The next time you walk down the street, take a good look at every face you pass. In your mind say Christ died for you--That slob. That phony. That crook. That saint. That fool. Christ died for you. Take and eat this in remembrance that Christ died for you."

Jesus said "This is my body" _after_ he broke the bread.

Bread: broken - separated - crushed - crumbled - sliced
        pulled apart - torn - ripped - mangled - in pieces

Jesus gave it to the disciples

                    betrayers - deserters - deniers: _all_
                    each in distinct ways.

And Jesus said, "Take, eat, this is my body which is _broken_ for you."

Shortly thereafter he entered the garden and there uttered his heartrending prayer: Father,

                    Must I drink this cup? It's so bitter.
                    Do I have to? Can't I let it pass?
                    Must I suffer so?

And Jesus' will and the Father's continued as one--_He was broken_.

Remember when Jesus Christ knew brokenness? We want to hurry past "Good Friday" and get to Easter Sunday. For, Sunday includes joy and celebration. We tend to blot out the end of Jesus' human life. We turn our heads when watching films about crucifixion, when the centurians pound the nails through the hands and feet of Jesus. We suddenly become weak-kneed. Our stomachs turn. As we put our hands over our faces, we grimace and say, "Oh, I can't handle that. Tell me when it's over."

In our culture we have great difficulty coping with pain and death--as a people and as a culture. We attempt to drive the crucifixion from our consciousness. But: He - was - broken. That makes all the difference in the world. That speaks volumes.

And we who have been broken, or we who _are_ broken, or we who are being broken feed deeply when we come to the communion table. We partake of the bread and hear the words: "Take, eat, this is my body which was broken for you."

You might ask, Where is the joy? Where is the celebration?
                    You speak only of sorrow and brokenness.

Gibran, in _The Prophet_, reminds us that joy and sorrow are inter-connected. Joy and sorrow go hand in hand. "The deeper that sorrow carves into your being, the more joy you can contain." Some of you might say,

"Joy is greater than sorrow," while others counter, "No, sorrow is the greater." But I say unto you, they are inseparable.

Mother Teresa has dedicated her life to giving help to the "poorest of the poor." This she bases on belief that we meet Christ in the poor. The poor die with dignity. Her helpers, too, feel that in feeding and bathing lepers, they are giving service to Christ. I have a friend who met Mother Teresa, who saw her in person and heard her speak. He said her face radiated joy.

I don't like stench, dirt, filth, disease, poverty, pain, heartbreak. Neither do I value TV commercials that emphasis every type of little ache, pain, or discomfort, for which relief is but a minute or pill away if you take the product advertised. The assumption seems to be that our highest goal is a life of ease and comfort. We are to be cushioned--free of pain and happy. But, that's not necessarily joy.

I heard the only woman school superintendent in Ohio share her pilgrimage with fifth and sixth grade girls contemplating new careers. Things were rough for her: tough - unjust - unfair. Whenever she was troubled or discouraged, her husband comforted her not with pity but by reminding her: "No one ever said it would be easy."

When we inquire, Why does this have to happen to me?, we do well to reflect. That comes close to New Testament theology of the cross. Jesus implies: I never said faithfulness would be easy.

I never said faithfulness would be free of pain.

I never said you would be exempt from suffering because of
    your solid faith or because you are good or right.

Some religions and expressions of faith suggest that. Some urge withdrawal from pain by spiritual concentration, as though the world and its sorrow were not worth our attention. Christianity neither denies the reality of pain and evil, nor withdraws from it. It neither resolves the problem nor explains it away.

The good news is that Jesus meets us in our suffering,
                                    in our brokenness.

Jesus the Christ directs us beyond easy solutions and explanations. The alternative offered implies: "We can manage somehow, if we put our pain together--you and I."

HE WAS BROKEN.

Because he was broken, we know we are loved, accepted, and precious. So we reach out to other aching, limping persons, and see in them the image of Christ.

ELSIE MILLER preached this sermon on the first Sunday of Lent, when the Lorraine Avenue Mennonite Church, Wichita, Kansas where she co-pastors, observes communion.

Messages of the Risen Christ
Sally Schreiner

A good way to look at the forty days between Jesus' resurrection and ascension is to contrast them with the forty days preceeding his crucifixion.

Those forty days were characterized by <u>preparation</u>, <u>confrontation</u>, and <u>consequences.</u> Jesus was preparing himself and his disciples for the trials ahead in a number of ways: turning toward Jerusalem, prophesying what was to come, teaching during the Last Supper, and praying in the Garden of Gethsemene. Jesus' confrontations were aimed in a number of directions. He confronted the "established orders" in his dialogues with the scribes and Pharisees, his challenge of Sabbath observances, and his interactions with Herod and Pilate during his trial. He also confronted the expectations of his followers concerning the kind of Messiah he was to be and how he would establish his reign. These confrontations led to swift and dramatic consequences: Jesus' arrest, trial, crucifixion, and burial. The forty days end in terrible suffering, bitter defeat, and unfulfilled hopes.

But resurrection followed--everything was turned around. Suddenly, the end becomes a beginning. The confronting powers which were in control are baffled and defeated. The preparation--the teachings about suffering, death, rising from the dead--all begin to make sense.

We have a risen Christ whose appearances are chronicled in six or more stories in the four Gospels and Acts. He spent the next forty days in a variety of ways, appearing to a variety of followers. Combining his messages into one is difficult because he was speaking to different needs and orientations of his followers. I am aware that you, too, are followers with different needs and different orientations. Therefore, as you hear my account of his messages to his diverse hearers, try to decide what messages the Risen Christ is speaking to you--in your distinctness, as you journey.

One message recorded in Luke 24:13-32 tells of the two disciples on the road to Emmaus. I characterize them as students of current events—observers and political analysts. They observe the events of the times and draw conclusions, but their understanding of these events is very limited. To them, Jesus says: You foolish men, "See me."

You are so into your own interpretation of events that you don't recognize who walks beside you. You don't see God's will fulfilled in Christ's suffering. Your perception only goes so far—open your eyes. Is there more to reality than what you are seeing? How is God's purpose being fulfilled right under your very nose, right beside you? Recognize your blindness so that I can teach you, so that I can reveal my nearness to you.

Another message, John 20:24-29, reports one of Jesus' two appearances to the eleven disciples in the locked upper room. This is the first time Thomas sees Christ. Thomas is the down-to-earth type who dwells in the realm of concrete physical detail, facts and evidence. I picture him as practical, solid, earthy and much given to saying, "I'll have to see it to believe it." To him, Christ says, "Have faith in me." Take a risk, Thomas, a leap out into the unknown. I'm willing to meet you where you are right now and let you put your hands on the proof you seek. But, hey, how about growing in belief? How about trusting me on the basis of my promises and not my physical presence? Jesus could have written him off for failing the test of belief. But, no, he shows understanding toward lack of comprehension. At the same time, he prods all followers to embrace greater fullness of truth.

John 21:1-19 records what I think is the climactic appearance of Jesus. This account focuses Peter, the man of actions, the impulsive, blunt, and spontaneous fellow. He doesn't waste a lot of time thinking or analyzing. His motto might read, "If it feels right, do it. If it needs saying, say it." As we look at his conversation with Christ on the beach, what is going on?

Christ's central message to Peter is "Love me." But why does he say it to him three times? One reason might be to give Peter three chances to clear his conscience of the three times he denied Christ. Another explanation is that Peter was thick-headed. If Jesus wanted the message to get through, he needed to repeat it. If you neglect someone you honestly care for, chances are you will be impressed by repeated calls to clarify your stance.

What then is the message? "Do you love me more than all else?" This is the fundamental question. He follows by saying, in essence, "Okay, then here's how you can show it to me: Feed my lambs. Tend my sheep. Feed my sheep." Loving always preceeds doing. Authentic love persists in spite of the consequences. Jesus concludes: "Follow me." This resembles his first recorded words to Peter. The journey continues. Motivation for following and feeding is love, all-out love for Jesus.

Matthew 28:16-20 expresses Jesus' great commission to all disciples. These are his final instructions, the marching orders, delivered to those who have been spectators in the stands as he has played out his battle with the forces of evil and death.

SALLY SCHREINER

This group of disciples (which spans all time to include us as well) can be likened to the fans who left the game during the last quarter before the time clock ran out, because the home team was doing so abysmally that there was no way they'd pull it out of the bag at the last minute ...But hold everything! Even after all the fans had deserted the stadium, the home team won. Come back and see for yourself. It seems unbelievable but it's true. We won! Hey, it's time to celebrate. Run out and tell everyone you know about this unbelievable victory. It's their victory too.

That's the way it is with Jesus' resurrection and ascension. The Risen Christ's final earthly message is "Witness about me." The Messiah has come. I've fulfilled the promise of the law and the prophets. All authority has been given to me. Death cannot hold me. You have nothing more to fear. Your sins are forgiven. Eternal life is yours. Celebrate. Don't hold this good news to yourself. Tell everyone. And one more thing, "I'm with you always." No more good-byes. I won't come to you in the bodily form you've been able to hear, see, and touch. But I'll put my Spirit within you--thus spreading myself further than has yet been possible.

Let's quickly review the central messages of Christ coming from these incidents: See me.
                  Have faith in me.
                  Love me.
                  Witness about me.

These are messages from the risen Christ to his followers in the forty days of ascension following resurrection--messages tailored to different followers. Probably several of these speak directly to you as well.

The good news is that Jesus was right: the Spirit is with us always. We continue to receive messages tailored to our personal needs. Let's reflect together in silence and listen for Divine truth. What are Christ's messages to us: individually and corporately?

SALLY SCHREINER delivered this sermon April 18, 1982, on the Sunday after Easter, to the informal Pilgrims Mennonite Church at Akron, Pennsylvania. She is Assistant Director of the U.S. Program of MCC, administering the Voluntary Service Program.

Justice

A LITANY OF CONFESSION
Written by Gayle Gerber Koontz

Leader: Compassionate and Holy God, we confess that we have often selected
and read biblical texts in ways which have kept women from becoming full and responsible members of this family of faith.

Congregation: We have often failed to value the insights and wisdom of
the women of God as highly as the men of God.

Leader: We are trapped and alienated by language.

Congregation: We believe that You are neither male nor female, but our
expressions are inconsistent. Or, we notice when our hymns
and scriptures do not use inclusive language, but we tire
of constantly making adjustments.

Leader: We are trapped and alienated by stereotypes.

Men: We have struggled against cultural attitudes and practices which
link maleness with the ability and willingness to use violence...

Women: ...and femaleness with weakness and fear.

Men: But we have not always been able to act as if gentleness and weeping
were masculine.

Women: And we have too often excused ourselves from following your call,
perceiving ourselves as more helpless than we are.

Leader: We have tasted the fruits and bitterness of power in relationships.

Men: We have pressed ourselves to compete by working long and hard. We
have expected wives and secretaries to serve us. We have defined
women as sexual objects.

Women: We have learned to value physical attractiveness and to use flat-
tery and surface compliance to manipulate men. We have seen husbands, male friends, and sons as means to power and prestige.

Congregation: We have been blind to the problems of women outside our
congregation and community--women of color, elderly and
single parent women struggling with inadequate incomes,
battered women, and women with little choice about pregnancy.

Leader: Forgive us, God of Jesus Christ, who gave yourself in love. Teach
us so to love one another.

Congregation: Make us one in your spirit.

GAYLE led the Assembly Mennonite Church, Goshen, Indiana, in this litany
on February 27, 1983.

The Words of Worship
Mary R. Schertz

Last Sunday,
   with Gayle leading us,
      we confessed, as a congregation
   that "we are trapped and alienated by language.
This morning,
   in our first hour,
      we experimented
   with the language of our worship.
We, who are used to enjoying
   the inclusive language for people
      in our Assembly Songbook,
   struggled, this morning,
      to adapt the more traditional
      Mennonite hymnal
      to our awakening sense of
      justice.
Also, in some of the songs we sang
   we changed the male pronouns
   which referred to God,
      to female ones.
We worshipped a God
   imaged as "she" and "her."
I'm guessing--
   that as we sit together here,
      one congregation,
         one people gathered,
            in the name of the one
            Christ,

we have many different emotions,
   many different feelings
      about our morning's worship.
Some of us may have come
   to this time of worship
      with a sense of relief,
      relaxation.
We may have experienced
   the morning as freedom--
   freedom to worship
      without being irritated
         or left lonely
      by exclusive language.
Others of us may have come
   to this time of worship
      with a sense of anxiety.
Some of the images used
   in our service
   may have jolted us,
      or left us with nagging questions.
Some of us may be feeling
   implicitly, if not explicitly,
      criticized by this emphasis
         on inclusive language.
We may be asking ourselves--
   "What's wrong with the way I talk?"
   "What's wrong with calling God
         Father?" or

75

MARY R. SCHERTZ

"What's so inclusive about
    calling God 'she'?"
The issues of inclusive language
    are sensitive ones
The way we talk is a very personal,
    intimate part of us.
    With words, we reveal who we are
        our thoughts
            our dreams
                our creativity
                    our questions
                our needs
                our incompetencies
            our prejudices.
Because language is so personal
    we don't talk about the way
        we use words
        very often.
In fact, unless we create some
    distance
by using some academic discipline
    such as philosophy
        or linguistics
        or theology,
we find the topic of language
    barely socially acceptable.
If we were to line up the kinds of
    corrections
    we offer each other
    with a question such as
        "Do you know your slip is
            showing?"
        on one end of the continuum
    and a question such as
        "Have you thought about changing
            the brand of deodorant you use?"
        on the other end--
The issues of language
    would probably
        fall somewhere in the middle.
At least, I don't know about you
    but I'm apt to get defensive
        if someone critisizes the way I
            pronounce words,
        let alone if someone says
            my language is sexist, racist,
                elitist.
So, in talking about language,

we need to remember
    and respect its personal nature.
We need to remember that
    language is a form of intimacy--
        and as with other forms of
            intimacy--
                there is potential therin
                    for brutality as well as
                    gentleness.
I would ask
    of all of us this morning
        that we be gentle with each
            other.
One way to do that,
    I suggest,
        is to keep in mind
            an image of faithfulness
                as a journey, a process.
Where I am,
    on the matters of inclusive
        language,
        as on other matters,
    is less important than where I am
        going.
Place
    matters less than direction.
I'll use Millard Lind as an example:
    most of us know who he is;
        many of us love him dearly
    and besides, at the moment,
        he is too far away to be embar-
            rassed
        by anything I might say.
Millard, of course, has been teaching Old Testament at the Seminary
for a goodly number of years. The
concept of what he calls the "family
of man" is central to his teaching
and dear to his heart.
    Well, when seminary women began
raising the issues of inclusive
language, Millard listened.
    And tried to change--
        not so much because he agreed
    with the "inherent rightness of
    the feminist cause"
        but because he genuinely cared
about his women students.

76

So he was willing
    to try to remember to say
"the human family,"
    and to ask pardon
for the times he forgot!
What is really more important?
    Where a person is?
    or how that person is moving?
--So
    With the need to be gentle in mind
    with the image of faithfulness as
    a journey
        we are making together in mind...
Let us consider
    two parts of this business
    of inclusive language in our
    worship.
These parts are:
    1) Language we use to talk about
        people.
    2) Language we use to talk to/
        about God.
(A third area we might keep in mind
for the discussion period is whether
our particular believers' church
perspective has any special insight
with which to work at these
questions.)
I. First, let's consider the lang-
        uage we use to talk about people.
    In many ways there isn't a lot to
    say about this particular aspect
    of the worship language issue in
    this setting. A number of years
    ago a committee worked through
    our Assembly Songbook
        - changing words such as "man-
            kind" to "people"
        - the exclusive singular "he"
            to the inclusive plural "they."
We have also, in this gathering,
    made a conscious and fairly consis-
    tent effort
    to say "men and women"
        "he or she" and so forth...
    in our worship leading, our sermons,
    and prayers.
I sense, at least, that we generally

agree
that such usage
    is not only more fair
        but more concrete and accurate.
The question on which we may not
    agree, however,
is: how much effort is this cause
        worth?
Changing our language
    is a constant and tiring task,
    and it has its own awkwardnesses.
    Shall I sing the exclusive term in
        a particular favorite hymn?
    Shall I not sing that phrase?
    Shall I change the exclusive word
        to an inclusive one?
        Shall I then sing as loudly on
        that word as I'm singing on
        the rest of the words?
And what about the person next
to me?
    If I'm sitting next to Marlin
    in the seminary chapel and he
    sings the inclusive word while I
    sing the exclusive one (as has
    happened), then I feel dumb. If
    I change the exclusive term to an
    inclusive term while the person
    next to me sings the exclusive
    term, then I feel critical and
    "holier-than-thou!"
And if we care about words
    and care about making these
    changes
    with some amount of grace and
    style,
    then the task is compounded!
Maybe we should all just admit
    that we're tired and frustrated!
But the question remains...
    is it worth the effort?
And I'd like to suggest, yes.
    For two reasons:
    1) First, there are so many in-
        justices in this world before
        which we are largely helpless
        --the threat of nuclear war,
            the population explosion in

77

Asia,
 hungry people in Africa.
Using language with care and fairness
 is one tangible, possible way
   to create justice in the space
   around us.
And that's no small thing.
2) Secondly, there are times
 when taking care with language
   matters a <u>lot</u>.
 A couple of years ago
   I attended a seminary class in
   which the teacher referred to
   ministers as male 173 times
   and to ministers as people or
   women exactly 0 times.

 There <u>would</u> have been a time in my
 life when I wouldn't have heard
 what was happening with the language and so would not have been
 bothered.
Now - after undergoing a solid process
 of gift-discernment, a process I
 trust, I feel more secure in my
 concept of myself as a minister
 and could probably handle that
 classroom situation with some
 equanimity.
The point is that, at that terribly
vulnerable time, that particular use
of exclusive language was destructive
to my sense of self, to my sense of
being called to the ministry. At that
moment, in that classroom, I really
wondered if the church had any room
for me and my gifts.

I simply think that since the one
 in whose name we gather
   - cared about creating justice
   around him
   - and cared for people
     in their weakness,
     their vulnerabilities,
     as well as in their strength,
so ought we.
Including all people
 in the ways we talk

is not only worth the effort,
 but a part of discipleship.
II. The second part of our consideration this morning is the
  question of God-language.
 I sense that we may disagree more
on this question than on the question of inclusive language for
humans. So, let's try to define
what is at stake here.
 I think Virginia Mollencott has
summarized the problem that masculine God-language poses for women
who are choosing not to be defined
by the patriarchal context in which
we live.
She says:
"It is difficult for women who
value being women to be 'clothed a
new in God's image' when God is de-
picted almost exclusively as
masculine."
Can I really deep down
 with all my heart and being
   <u>believe</u> that I am indeed
     created in the very image
       of God
if God is almost always
 a "He"
 or the "Father"?
Well, as Mollencott says,
 <u>it is difficult</u>.
A friend of mine
 describes the first time she saw
the painting of the Black Messiah
 as one of <u>the</u> powerful events of
 her life.
She says that as
 she stood
   looking up into the face of
     the Black Jesus,
   the tears streamed down her face
and she thought,
 yes, Jesus knows how I feel;
   Jesus knows what being black
   means.
   Jesus is black, too.
At that moment

78

she knew herself to be
  a fully beloved member
    of the family of God.
Imagining the feminine God
  a "she" like me;
    seeing God in the faces of my sisters
helps me know
    that I too am a fully beloved
                        treasured
                        cherished
    member of the family of God.
I will not soon forget
    the first time
      I heard someone name God "Mother"
      and pray to her in public.
The tingling warmth of that moment
    is a part of my knowing
      I really do belong here.
For that reason,
  I think we need
    to make space
      in our worship life
      to imagine the feminine God
      and to call upon her.
Because women as well as men
    are created in the image of God.
Because if God is Father, then God
    is also Mother.
Just how do we go about making space
    for a feminine God?
Do we worship God-He and God-She
    on alternate Sundays?
Do we worship God-She for the next
    2,000 years on the assumption that
    equal time is basic to fairness?
Do we invite the men to sing "He" and
    the women to sing "She"?
Well, I'd like to suggest a solution
    that's a bit more modest
      than any of those proposals
    somewhat less mechanistic,
    and, in my humble opinion,
      somewhat more fun!
First, we need to remind ourselves that
    the image of God as Father is a lot
      more important to Western theology
        than it is to Biblical theology.
We also need to remind ourselves that

one of the earliest Biblical
concerns was the prohibition
against false gods.
The Hebrew people were not unmind-
    ful that we can construct false
gods
with words as well as clay or stone.
    One of the ways they worked at
this problem was their refusing
to say the name of God. To this
day, the pronunciation of "Yahweh"
one of the Hebrew names for God
is a pure guess. The name was not
ever said and since in the Hebrew
language the vowels were not
written, the pronunciation is forever lost to us.
However, Refusing to name God
    did not mean the Hebrews did not
      talk about God.
    They used a wealth of metaphors
      to describe the divine.
    A gander through the Psalms
      yields descriptions of God
        as a cup, a bird,
          a rock, shield,
            horn of salvation,
          a storm, a lamplighter,
        a midwife, a shepherd,
        a warrior, a king,
    and a gardener.
The Hebrews seemed
  to have had some notion
      that the divine-human relation-
      ship is both rich and complex
    and that no one image can poss-
    ibly suffice,
      to convey this richness and
      complexity.
The Hebrew response to the human
tendency to grasp God in a single
concept was to create many ideas
about God.
There's a description
  of the Hebrew theologian
    that I like:
"A Hebrew sucked the juice out
  of each metaphor as he used it,

79

and threw the skin away at once."
The way of the Hebrews in their poetry
  and later
the way of Jesus
  in the parables and the stories
was to pile
  image upon image,
absorbing the richness of each
  and letting them go to
  create new images,
not insisting upon any one image
  as the image of God,
not absolutizing any one image.
Perhaps the most reverent way
  to talk about God
    is to create our images
      and to hold them loosely.
Perhaps one of the
  ways we can truly worship is
To create an image
  to struggle to say clearly
    and with passion
  God is to me like...
and then to let that image go.
To hold onto any image too tightly
  whether God as father,
        God as mother
  is to grasp God,
    to box God into a single idea
  and, at least, a form of idolatry.
I'd like to suggest
  that we make space for
    ourselves to image God as
    feminine
  and participate
    in that one small way
    in the healing of both women
      and men
    in righting the injustices of a
    patriarchal society
by holding all our images of God
  important as they are,
  developed over years of religious
  experience
    as they are,
a little less tightly.
  Let's see what richness these new

images can bring to us.
  We might be surprised.
I have been.
Perhaps
  an illustration of this process
    might be helpful
Growing up in central Illinois
  means growing up under a big sky.
Spending days running through
  cow pastures and down along the
  creek
and evenings
watching the sun set from the crooked
  branch of the Jonathan tree.
The ever-changing sky became a
  companion,
  a part of my sense of well-being
    a part of my delight in my
    world.
As I came to know God,
  light became an important symbol
    for God.
But when I spent a year in Philadelphia, I found that my black friends
  had different feelings about my
  simple equations of light with God
  and good.
And for very good reasons--
  Because dark-skinned people have
  been oppressed by light-skinned
  people,
the image of God as light
  is not adequate.
  It is sometimes painful
    for dark-skinned people.
So I needed to think also
  about the ways God is like
  darkness.
  The simple equation of darkness
  with evil and light with good
  was no longer adequate
  for me or, even true.
I still like to think
  about God when I watch the
  sun set.
But thinking about God as the
  darkness into which the light

fades and from which the
light emerges
has enriched/ not depleted/ my
concept of God as light.
I'd simply like to close
by reading one of my
favorite images--
an image in which God is a place
a place we usually refer to
with feminine pronouns,
a place where no one is hurting anymore--
Zion...
(Isaiah 35:5-10)
Then the eyes of the blind shall be opened,
and the ears of the deaf unstopped;
then shall the lame man leap like a hart,
and the tongue of the dumb sing for joy.
For waters shall break forth in the wilderness,
and streams in the desert;
the burning sand shall become a pool,
and the thirsty ground springs of water;
the haunt of jackals shall become a swamp,
the grass shall become reeds and rushes.
And a highway shall be there,
and it shall be called the Holy Way;
the unclean shall not pass over it,
and fools shall not err therein.
No lion shall be there,
nor shall any ravenous beast come up on it;
they shall not be found there
but the redeemed shall walk there,
And the ransomed of the Lord shall return,
and come to Zion with singing,
with everlasting joy upon their heads;
they shall obtain joy and gladness,
and sorrow and sighing shall flee away.

MARY R. SCHERTZ gave this sermon at Assembly Mennonite Church, Goshen,
Indiana, on March 6, 1983, helping the congregation pursue one of its
goals for the year. Mary has completed her MDiv degree at AMBS and will
likely pursue grad work in biblical studies or theology in the future.

A New Heaven and a New Earth

Dorothy A. Friesen

Hebrews 11
Isaiah 65
II Peter 3:13

The Bible is essentially the story of the people of God and the decisions and actions they made to be faithful to the vision of what God wants
for the world. But not only their decisions and actions are recorded in
the Bible; also important is the action of God in their lives. The 11th
chapter of Hebrews lists some of the stories of the people of God.
    The writer of Hebrews introduces the list by saying:
        To have faith is to be sure of the things we hope for,
        to be certain of the things we cannot see."
By their faith people of ancient times won God's approval. The rest of the
chapter is filled with the summaries of the stories of the Old Testament.
    Hebrews 11:7 records: "It was faith that made Noah hear God's warning
about things in the future that he could not see. He obeyed God and built
a boat in which he and his family were saved." Noah had a vision that his
neighbors did not share. His reference point was different from his neighbors' who made fun of him. He was an oddball in the community.
    The story of Moses we read from verse 23 and following:
        It was faith that made the parents of Moses hide him for three
        months after he was born. They saw that he was a beautiful child
        and they were not afraid to disobey the king's order. It was
        faith that made Moses, when he had grown up, refuse to be called
        the son of the king's daughter. He preferred to suffer with
        God's people rather than enjoy sin for a little while. He reck-
        oned that to suffer scorn for the Messiah was worth far more
        than all the treasures of Egypt, for he kept his eyes on the
        future reward.

Moses' parents took risks because they held values other than blind obedience to the ruler's orders. Now Moses could have used his power as a prince (his power as president of the corporation) to get things done on behalf of his people. But the Bible tells us he had a different value system. He was certain that the treasures of Egypt, which his neighbors counted valuable, were less than the vision of the future which God has for the people. Despite the military might of the Egyptian Pharoah, Moses' faith was not attacked there. We read in verse 27, "It was faith that made Moses leave Egypt without being afraid of the king's anger. As though he saw the invisible God, he refused to turn back."

In verse 31 we read about Rahab:

> It was faith that kept the prostitute Rahab from being killed with those who disobeyed God, for she gave the Israelite spies a friendly welcome.

Rahab saw something her neighbors did not see. She was ready to risk her life, not just for the Israelite spies, but for the vision of a different society, of change occurring in Jericho at that point. Her action today might be equivalent to housing KGB agents, a serious matter in the growing climate of hostility between the United States and the USSR.

Each of these people seized the moment. They made decisions which opened the possibility for a new kind of life which said <u>No</u> to death. They are our cloud of witnesses as we seek to move towards the new heaven and the new earth. Why could these people turn their backs on society as it was and take risks for a new vision? From where did that vision of a new heaven and new earth come? The description threads its way through both the Old and New Testaments, but a passage which captures the vision in a few words is Isaiah 65:17-22.

> The Lord says I am making a new heaven and a new earth. The events of the past will be completely forgotten. There will be no weeping there, no calling for help. Babies will no longer die in infancy and all people will live out their life span. People will build houses and get to live in them. They will not be ruled by someone else. They will plant vineyards and enjoy the wine; it will not be drunk by others. The people will fully enjoy the things that they have worked for.

But we know we are far from the new heaven and new earth. In the Philippines, for example, two-thirds of all children under six suffer from second and third degree malnourishment, according to World Health Organization statistics. Though we have the promise that all people will live out their life span, seventy-four out of one thousand children die before their first birthday. People will get to live in the houses they build is the promise. But in the Philippines people are driven from their land to make way for agribusiness--bananas, pineapples, coconut, and sugar that come to our country. People are promised they will drink the wine from their vineyards, but they work for less than two dollars a day for Mattel who makes Barbie dolls and Ford who makes fenders in the Philippines.

Such big problems and so far away. How can we do anything? I want to share with you the story of God's people in the Philippines and in

83

Warman, Saskatchewan, Canada. I want to share how their faithfulness to the vision of the new heavens and new earth intersected, although they are twelve thousand miles away and don't know each other personally.

The story begins in Warman, Saskatchewan where Mennonite farmers had had dairies for a few generations. Eldorado Nuclear Corporation, a crown corporation in Canada, planned to build a uranium refinery on some of that dairy land. A development agency began buying options for the land. Some Mennonites sold, although they did not know what would be developed in their area. When they found out that uranium would be refined there, they began to raise questions. They asked about the safety of the plant, about how the waste would affect the water in the nearby Saskatchewan River which they used to irrigate their lands. They asked about the pollution of their drinking water, which came from underground water supplies. They also knew that uranium is an indispensable part of nuclear weapons and nuclear reactors.

Premier Blakeney of Saskatchewan told them that to withhold uranium for nuclear development in Third World countries was immoral. It doomed people in those countries to subsistence living. The people of Warman wanted to know what having nuclear reactors would mean for people in the Philippines. They had heard that the Philippine and Canadian governments were talking about the sale of uranium for the newly-constructed nuclear plant in the Philippines. They wrote to us while we were working with MCC in the Philippines. Because of their questions, we went to visit the little town of Morong just north of Manila, the capital city of the Philippines.

There, we found fishermen, farmers, and fear. The nuclear plant is being built between two earthquake vaults on the slope of a volcanic mountain in an area where the tidal waves are pounding. Eighty percent of the town income comes from fishing. Small bangus fingerlings, a favorite food, lived in the streams around the town. Because of the construction of the plant, the streams were muddied and the fingerlings died. Thirty-six families have already been moved off their land to make way for the plant, some without just compensation.

The people of Morong, like the people of Warman, were not told about the plant. They found out by accident. They raised questions and asked for public meetings to explain what this plant would mean in their lives. Sixty uniformed military men attended the meeting and intimidated the citizens. A Methodist pastor who raised questions about where the waste would be stored was told by a military officer at the meeting, "Why are you asking so many questions? You must be a subversive." A worker in the plant who asked too many questions was arrested, tortured, and killed. Some of the core people of the opposition to the plant became very afraid and disappeared into the hills. One sympathizer, who had not been active in the organization, was picked up and killed.

We also found in Morong a basic Christian community. The base Christian communities are an exciting part of Filipino church life. They are essentially groups of ordinary people getting together to read the Bible, pray, and take action together in economic or social projects. The meeting we attended lasted from seven in the evening until late into the night.

The passage the Filipinos were studying came from II Peter 3. They focused on the 13th verse, "but we wait for what God has promised, new heavens and a new earth where justice will be at home." This verse brought a lot of excited discussion. The promise of the new heavens and a new earth contrasted with the reality of what was happening in Morong. However, the people did not focus only on their problems in Morong. They also talked about aboriginal land in Australia which was being taken away from native peoples because of the uranium in those areas.

In January of 1980 the Canadian federal government held hearings on placing a uranium refinery in Warman, Saskatchewan. The concerned citizens of Warman asked for some time within the hearings to discuss the moral questions. The federal panelists said that wasn't necessary. Though the hearings were supposed to be technical--on ecological and socioeconomic benefits--the people of Warman turned the hearings into a moral and ethical discussion. They united to say No to death.

Old men, housewives who had never spoken in public before, and small children stood to give their testimony of peace. Many of the people quoted the Bible and said, "We are a people of peace. We used to show our disagreement with war by refusing to send our sons. However, life has become more complex. Now the uranium we find in this area will be used for nuclear weapons to kill people. We say No to this."

Fathers talked about being stewards of the land, having received this land developed by their grandfathers and wishing to pass it on to their sons and grandsons in good condition. Students from the Swift Current Bible Institute and the Canadian Mennonite Bible College returned home, though they were in the middle of the semester, to support their families. One group brought a solar oven right in front of the chairman and through a one act drama proclaimed their willingness to change their lifestyle in order to find more peaceable ways to supply energy. One farm wife brought a tin of milk, a glass of wheat, and strawberries and placed them in front of the chairperson of the panel saying, "This is what grows on our land; we want to continue to raise it."

Why were the people of Warman able to say No to the uranium refinery out of self-interest and in behalf of people in the Philippines who are enduring great suffering because of capital intensive projects like the nuclear plant? The community of Warman holds many traditional Mennonite values. They are a peaceable community. They concentrate on church life. They meet together, as do churches all over North America.

In the past they did not know that they would be challenged by this uranium refinery. They simply tried to build a healthy church life which connected the demands of the gospel with their everyday social and economic life. Here were people who had thought about ethical implications of the gospel. There were also people in this community who had the courage to raise the issue and keep at it when a majority of the community was non-supportive or still confused about the meaning of a refinery for their area. Whereas over seventy-five percent of the community now stood against the refinery, at the beginning of this process, only a few spoke out.

DOROTHY A. FRIESEN

    We have read about the cloud of witnesses in Hebrews 11. The people
of Warman belong on this list. By faith Noah, by faith Moses, by faith
Rahab and by faith the people of Warman spoke out against death. They
spoke as a people of peace. They witnessed to life. Their witness will
support us as we stand against the pull of the old earth and heavens,
against the security of the familiar.
    The example of the cloud of witnesses goes before us and the spirit of
God goes with us. May God give us all the courage and strength to proclaim
the new heaven and the new earth in our lives, in the decisions which
affect us locally and which will at some point inevitably intersect with
situations faced by our Third World sisters and brothers.

DOROTHY A. FRIESEN preached this sermon at Stirling Avenue Mennonite Church
in Kitchener, Ontario in 1980. She is coordinator of SNAPSES in Chicago,
where she lives. This organization attempts to make connections with Third
World people, working with crafts and networking with political effort.

Ballast, Buckets, Billows
Nancy Kerr

When the leader says: "The peace of God be with you!"
   And you respond: "And with your spirit,"
What does that mean?

If we greet friends: Shalom!
   And they respond: Shalom!
What are we saying?

In Jesus' time and in Israel today "Shalom" starts and ends a conversation. But what does Shalom <u>mean</u>? English fails to encompass all the meaning that "Shalom" has in Hebrew. Although "Peace" comes close, truly no one English word will do. For, Shalom means many kinds of peace (even some we don't usually include in peace).
Shalom means the peace that comes from :
   Harmony, not discord;
   Justice, not oppression;
   Health, not dis-ease;
   Calm order, not chaos;
   Love (in the Pauline sense of I Cor. 13);
   Security - Friendship - Well-being.
<u>All</u> of that is what we want for someone whom we greet: Shalom!
   Shalom! (Respond: Shalom!)
   God intends Shalom for all of us children. And so the Prince of Peace was sent to establish it. Jesus says, "My peace I leave with you." (John 14:27), and "in me you have peace." (John 16:33)
   "If you love me, keep my commandments.
   If you keep my commandments, you will abide in my love.
   And I will send you a comforter, even the Spirit of Truth."
This is the Peace which passes all understanding.
   Shalom! (Shalom!)

Prophet Micah speaks of Shalom that is true religion:
    "God has shown you what is good:
     and what does the Lord require of you
        but to do justice, love kindness, and walk humbly with your God."
Isaiah 58:6-8 quotes God as saying:
    "The fast I choose is this:
        to loose the bonds of wickedness;
        to undo the thongs of the yoke;
        to let the oppressed go free;
        and to break every yoke."
This means to share your bread with the hungry;
              to bring the homeless into hour house;
              to clothe the naked;
              to not hide yourself from your family.
Then shall your light break forth like the dawn and your healing spring
up speedily. Your righteousness shall go before you. Then you shall call
and the Lord will answer; you shall cry and God will answer "Here I am."
    Jesus says: (Matthew 25:35-36) To inherit the Commonwealth of Peace
you must: give food to the hungry and drink to the thirsty,
              clothe the naked and visit the sick and go to those in prison.
In as much as you do it to one of the least of these, you do it to me."
    Shalom! (Shalom!)
    How do we get and give Shalom?
You know the Bible passages I've just quoted. If you reflect, you can recall ways in which you seek, make, and keep shalom. I suggest that for
what you are now doing, and for doing even more, one needs
    ballast, buckets, and billows.
    I want to use this ship talk to tie our head, hands, and heart into
what I think are some basic requirements for the Christian:
    Shalom-seeker, Shalom-maker, Shalom-keeper.
For peace is not passive! Peace in Hebrew is an action word. We are called
to be do-ers of God's peace, and not be hearers only (James 1:22).
    The following is a nautical story, with a salutary ending, and worthy
of all acceptation, for it is true. When my children were 12 and 16, a
friend let them take a sailboat out on Lake Winnepesaukee. They listened
to the instructions. Then they tried to put into practice what they'd been
told. At first, they stayed close to shore. But soon--too soon--they grew
confident and headed for open water. Ten minutes later I could still see
the sail, but I could no longer see them.
    Then the sail went over and the boat capsized!
    That moment was terrible for me. I saw that, in a few minutes, 16
years of my life's work could be lost. (Perhaps God feels the same way
about us when we get swept away or go down into the depths.) I am no sail-
or. There I was on shore. Helpless. I knew every second might count in
saving them from drowning. (Probably, God doesn't panic as this mother
did! Both children had life-saving skills.)
    But even as I ran for help, a friend in a motorboat had already put
out for where the Sunfish lay upended in the water. My friend found the

children hanging on to the boat (so the boat wouldn't be lost, they later
told me!) My friend directed the righting of the boat. Securing a tow
line, this friend took the children out of the water and brought them back
to me, safe and sound.

As Luke says in the God parables of chapter 15:
"There was great rejoicing when that which was lost was found."
Often, we get lost and need to be found.
In the ocean of this world, our life boats struggle
> to ride steady,
> to keep from going under,
> to find the breath to steer a course through the flotsam and the

jetsam. In order to bring Shalom to the shipwrecked, our life boats need
Ballast,   Buckets,   and Billows.
But first, we need a manual of instruction.

Richard and Donna had not spent enough time "learning the ropes."
They had not read the manual or pored over instructions. They needed practice at putting instructions into action.

Some of us set out on a life course
before we have really read the Bible,
before we have really learned its rules of living,
before we have had some practice at putting our faith into action.

Being a Christian is something like being a sailor. One must learn
and practice, and perhaps make some mistakes, before mastery is achieved.
Then one goes on learning, and doing, and being a better Christian, the
more one reads that manual of instruction, the Bible.

We'd better start with the Bible before we
> put down ballast
> pick up buckets, and
> puff out sails with billows.

BALLAST

Let's talk about putting down ballast. A sailboat, which has no hold
for ballast, is very unstable. It cannot weather a storm; even a little
gust will do you. (At least a gust is what my children blamed.) Rich and
Donna were using themselves for ballast, and that didn't work very well.
For the life course one might do better
> to be filled deep with an understanding of God;
> to take in as much as we can hold of God's way and will for us;
> to be weighed down, weighted, in God's being.
> God is our Rock and our stay. (Ps. 62:2);
> > a very present help in time of trouble (Ps. 46:1).
> Therefore, we will not fear
> > though the earth should change,
> > though the mountains shake in the heart of the sea;
> > though its waters roar and foam. (Ps. 46:2-3)

God must be our ballast if we are to sail a shalom course in this life,
> > if we are to ride out securely and steadfastly
> > > the turbulence and tempests which overtake us.

NANCY KERR

BUCKETS

No ship deep enough for a hold or sturdy enough to carry a load in this life can do without buckets (or, in this mechanized age, a bilge pump!) Sometimes the sea waves are high. Storms do come and, although we try to roll with the waves, the water sweeps over the deck and we are in danger of going down,

of being swept away.

We must get busy with buckets and bail out. We need buckets.

The woman at the well (John 4) said to Jesus: "Sir, the well is deep, and you have nothing with which to draw." No bucket. But Jesus said in effect, "I am the bucket." Ask of me.

Follow me.

Do what I do.

And you will have the bucket to draw up, bail out, fill, empty. Jesus can save us from drowning in the deeps of life. Jesus is our bucket.

But Jesus saves us in order that God's work may be done. We are saved to carry Shalom, to work peace, to bring justice. Paul describes us as being rescued to be ambassadors for Christ (II Cor. 5:16-21)

Buckets are a symbol of good works. Jesus began his ministry, his service, by announcing that there was good news for the poor, liberty for the captives, sight for the blind, and freedom for the oppressed. (Luke 4: 18, Isaiah 61:1-2, Isaiah 58:6)

Jesus' bucket is a busy one.

Our buckets must be busy too.

To steer a Peace Passage, a Shalom course,

you've got to have ballast, be weighted down with God's presence;
you've got to have buckets, to work as Jesus did;
   and you have to billow.

BILLOWS

A boat goes nowhere without power. In the days of clipper ships, the wind needed to billow the sails before a ship could move. (Today, of course, we have engines of immense power, whose wind is steam.)

The words of an old hymn come back to me: "When upon life's billows you are tempest tossed; When you are discouraged thinking all is lost." That describes a storm wind, but we need some wind in our sails to go! Billows symbolize the power of the Holy Spirit. The word for Spirit or wind, or air, or breath in Hebrew is "Ruah." Breath-of-Life or Holy-Spirit-Nurture suggest more than other traditional descriptions of the persons' of God female qualities. Ruah is, interestingly, a feminine word in Hebrew. (I don't know how the Holy Wind in English translations came to be neutered and referred to as "it.") However, the Holy Wind must billow our lives.

Many of us get hold of the ballast of God and the bucket of Jesus and forget to put up a sail to catch the billows. We forget to test the Holy Winds, to billow with the power of God's Spirit. But we need the power of the Holy Spirit to keep us going in the right direction,

on the right course,

at the right time.

When Jesus began his ministry of service, he said"The Spirit is upon me." Luke records that the Spirit also came upon Mary. In both events, the words of the spirit-filled person are words proclaiming Shalom liberation. John suggests, "It is the Spirit that gives Life." (6:63) We must billow with the Holy Spirit to move on a Shalom course.

How do we get and give Shalom? We start with the Bible as a good manual of instruction. If we utilize the presence of God,
the practice of Christ, and
the power of the Holy Spirit,
our lifeboats will have the ballast to ride steady,
the buckets to bail out or bring in, and
the billows of power:
to seek and to share the fullness of peace;
to end oppression, heal the sick, feed the hungry, liberate the captive,
to establish and maintain the Shalom commonwealth.

We Mennonites have, it seems to me, some more ballast and buckets in our Anabaptist heritage. We are grounded in a history that shows us how, in the Fellowship of the Faithful, to live out a peace ethic. Our ballast is the weight of worshippers in the 1500's working only love, who yet bore as did Christ the violence of the world's rejection. They gave love and received hate. They gave peace and received persecution. Our sense of Shalom grew because of Blaurock and Sattler,
because of Soentja and Elizabeth the Teacher,
because of all those early Mennonite Martyrs.

We also have the history of those buckets of hard work which drained the Vistula, the Molutschna, the Conestoga and made good land for farming. And there are the buckets of help Sophie Brown gave in China, Ella Bauman in India, and S. F. Haury with the Cherokee. Mennonite Mutual Aid, Mennonite Disaster Service, Mennonite Voluntary Service, Mennonite Central Committee: of such are the buckets for peace-making and peace-keeping
IN THE NAME OF CHRIST.

Surely the power of the Holy Spirit filled them with all knowledge of the loving, non-violent, peace that passes all understanding. That commitment to seek and serve shalom is a heavy treasure from our past. We are a peace people in the full sense of that word. Our course is to give love and avoid returning evil.

I John says: "This is the message which we have heard from the beginning, that we should love one another. By this we know love, that he laid down his life for us and we ought to lay down our lives for each other. And this is the commandment, that we should believe in Jesus Christ and love one another. All who keep his commandments abide in him and he in them. And by this we know that God abides in us by the Spirit which has been given us."

No one can love God and hate human beings.
Such a person is a liar.
For if we cannot love people who are visible,
how can we love God who is invisible?
So this commandment we have:

91

that those who love God must love the human family also.
And the Spirit is the witness, because the Spirit is Truth.
How do we get and give Shalom?
How do we pick up and pass along the peace that comes from:
  harmony - justice - health - order - security - love - well-being?
How can this be borne along in our lifeboats?
  With the ballast of God's presence,
        the buckets of Christ's example,
        the billows of the Spirit's power
we can be Shalom-seekers, Shalom-makers, Shalom-keepers.
Then God is in our head, our hands, our heart.
  Being anchored to God, we can act with Christ, oriented by the Spirit.
  Being bound in the Believers Church, we serve, in the name of Christ,
                            through the Fellowship of Faith.
  Being children of God, we follow God's Son in spirit-guided care for
                            each other.

Prayer: God of our being,
        In the love of Christ and by the direction of the Holy Spirit,
        Grant us peace (shalom)...and then
        Help us to give it away!
            Shalom!   (Shalom!)

NANCY KERR has preached this at several places in her work as coordinator
of PEACE, Peace Education as Campus Evangelism, a project of the General
Conference Mennonite church's Department of Higher Education. She is also
pastor of the Cincinnati Mennonite Fellowship.

92

The Blessing of Children
Mary A. Schiedel

When I see a newborn baby lying contently asleep in its basket or even
squirming and howling, I can't help but think of it as a very special gift
from God. The baby may look more beautiful a few weeks or months later,
but I am impressed--and I'm sure many of you mothers and fathers have been
too--at the new life that tiny infant possesses and at the almost overwhelming possibilities that lie ahead. A baby is so small, but so significant. At Christmas time we speak of God's gift of Jesus who was born as a
baby in Bethlehem. I thought of that in connection with Rebecca LeAnn
because she was born just three days before Christmas this year.

We get excited when a baby is born. Usually nobody knows exactly
what time of day or night the baby will arrive, but afterwards the news is
passed on quickly. It's good news--like when we heard that Chuck and
Alexis had their baby. Everybody hears about it--brothers and sisters,
grandparents, uncles and aunts, friends and relatives. And most of the
time, everyone is happy.

Strange, isn't it? The baby hasn't done anything yet to earn our
appreciation. It needs a lot of care, and considerable time before it becomes a person able to take care of most personal needs. A young child is
so dependent on Mother and Father. It couldn't survive without some primary care. If, for some reason, a mother can't keep and care for her child
others are often eager to adopt the responsibilities. To accept the child
as a gift of God. To open their lives to the blessing that a child or children bring into their home.

What are these blessings? I'm going to talk about some of them, and
you may easily think of more ways in which children enrich and add to our
lives.

Children, I realize that today I am going to talk <u>about</u> you, and that
is hardly even polite or fair. But I will try to talk directly <u>to</u> you at
times. You may want to listen also when it's about you. When I was young,

93

I remember learning to understand Pennsylvania Dutch because I thought my parents might be saying things I wasn't to hear. So I was determined to understand. Any way, you are welcome to listen.

Anyone who has lived with a baby knows what a difference its presence makes in a home. When Andrew was born, the announcement we sent out showed a clothesline of diapers with the message, "Times are changing--but not as much as we are."

The first blessing through children is that they change our lives. Through the first days or sleepless nights, that isn't easy. Along with those excited, joyful feelings at times of birth, there is already a mixture of some anxiety, or at least concern, about how well parents can care for that child. They must change their patterns of sleeping, for example, when the baby needs a feeding in the middle of the night. While this may last only a few weeks or months, it's a foretaste of what lies ahead-- sleepless nights for other reasons. Some may occur when a nine year old may be sick with measles and needs close attention. Or a 19 year old may be out late causing worry for a parent. Usually, the worry ends when the child recovers or the teenager returns or calls to explain the delay. The process of moving from the crib to the car involves a lot of change and growth, even painful adjustments for children and parents. But therein is blessing too.

A second source of blessing through children is their spontaneity and joy. Often just to be with them offers pleasure. That is, if we're ready to offer time and interest. A poster I have has a picture of a small boy on a tricycle and the words, "Of course children get in your way. But where are you going?" Probably all of us recall the feeling of reward from spending time with a child--just talking, or doing something that both enjoy. Children are often very understanding of adults. They know we like to be silly and play sometimes. They know what trying something difficult is like. And they accept parents who don't "know everything" after all. Sometimes, children, you help us to enjoy ourselves more, to have more fun. You bless our lives with your laughter, your funny jokes and riddles. You make us happy when you invite us to join you in play. We do well to reveal the child in each of us.

A third way that children bless adults is through needing us. Parents grow through responsible care and discipline of their children. Their need for some guidelines and boundaries, for some rules made and enforced in kindness, help adults change. One woman who teaches parenting courses at the YWCA was quoted in the K-W Record several years ago as saying, "No two year old is going to have an equal voice with me. Too much responsibility can be threatening to a child who may wonder whether the parents do care. That's why some children keep testing--just to see how far they can go."

I perceive that pre-schoolers and teenagers do test us. Although a two year old doesn't need an equal voice in making decisions, children do deserve an equal ear. They need us to listen to them and to understand how they're feeling about what is going on in their lives.

Children need adults to show them the way. Being aware of that need, they help us to become more mature. But not perfect. They easily see our

94

weaknesses. But they can know that we care enough about them to provide kind but firm discipline. To love them that much. I like the "Life is Too Short" list written by Doris Janzen Longacre. A couple of these are: "Life is too short not to hug your spouse and each of your kids everyday. Life is too short to put off improving relationships with the people we live with."

Fourth, children are a blessing and a gift from God because they teach us a lot about faith. A small child is trusting and dependent on the a- dults in his or her life. And as the child develops s/he learns self trust and trust in God. When Jesus was talking with his disciples about who would be valued in the kingdom of heaven, he called a child to join their circle and said, "Truly I say to you, unless you turn and become like children, you will never enter the kingdom of heaven. Whoever knows humility like this child is the greatest in the kingdom of heaven."

Children can model for us simple faith and trust in God. They remind us, when we don't know what to do, that depending on and trusting God is useful, that other people can be helpful too. Children encourage us to be honest; they see through pretense and insincerity. They hold fewer grudg- es against each other--in their eagerness to get back to playing together. Of course there are quarrels, jealousies, teasing and even cruelty. But there is often a willingness to admit mistakes, to forgive and forget. Children can teach us humility and trust.

You may easily be thinking of other ways in which children bless our lives; I want to speak of one more. I believe children are a blessing to all of us, and especially to the Church, because they prod us to think about and work for the future. If we believe life to be good--to be a gift from God--we want to offer the children of our homes and congregation opportunity to live out their lives with faith and freedom. Sometimes I think that bringing a child into our world today is an act of faith. I know that some young couples think seriously about that. It calls for a commitment to make the world, or our small part of it, a safe and worth- while place. It calls for us to work at major issues like nuclear dis- armament and to think beyond our immediate families. Children in our community and around the world deserve equal opportunity for adequate food, clothing, and housing. Equal opportunity for education and for learning to know and believe in a loving God.

Here, we work to provide secure homes and a loving church fellowship in which our children can grow and develop. I like to think that in some ways children belong to all of us in the church. We help each other find faith and work toward the future. Together, we confront uncertainty about the future.

What, then, can we pass on to the next generation that will be of most help? I would suggest that the most important dimension is our faith --faith in God that has inspired and sustained us in life. To picture the world 50 or 60 years from now is hard. But I do hope and pray that it will be a place where children can laugh and play and learn in safety and peace. I believe there will be opportunities for our children and our children's children to accomplish what would make us happy and proud. I

MARY A. SCHIEDEL

invite them to live out and pass on the faith to future generations.

Yes, children bless our lives, and we bless them. The impact goes both ways, even if a two year old doesn't have an equal voice or can't make some decisions. It's a two-way experience in that if children are to respect us, we must respect them too. We live and learn together.

I conclude with a quotation that reminds us of our task--at home, at work, and in the church--during and beyond a child's infancy.

Children Learn What They Live

If a child lives with criticism, s/he learns to condemn.
If a child lives with hostility, s/he learns to fight.
If a child lives with ridicule, s/he learns to be shy.
If a child lives with shame, s/he learns to feel guilty.
If a child lives with tolerance, s/he learns to be patient.
If a child lives with encouragement, s/he learns confidence.
If a child lives with praise, s/he learns to appreciate.
If a child lives with fairness, s/he learns justice.
If a child lives with security, s/he learns to have faith.
If a child lives with approval, s/he learns to like him/herself.
If a child lives with acceptance and friendship,
S/he learns to find love in the world.

(Pronouns adapted by editor.)

MARY A. SCHIEDEL preached this message during a service of child-parent dedication at Preston Mennonite Church, Ontario, where she had a one-year interim pastor assignment. Mary plans to continue full-time study at Waterloo Lutheran next year.

Beyond Winning
Rosie Epp

Mark 9:33-37; 10:35-45

For many of us, our weekends are filled with playing or watching baseball or other sports events. With these games come winners and losers, good feelings and bad.

Winning has become an important goal item in our society. Being the high scorer, the best piano player, the top executive, or the strongest nation have become incentives toward which we Americans strive. To win, to be number one, to be the best is a desire all of us experience.

Some time ago national TV pictured a well-known football coach as he hit an opposing player who had intercepted a pass and sealed the defeat of the coach's team. Winning had become so important to this coach that he hit a player out of anger and disappointment at not being able to achieve his goal of winning.

When the American hockey team won an Olympic gold medal over the Russians, the U.S. went into a collective spasm of jubilation, turning that victory into a triumph of God over atheism or capitalism over communism, and punishment of Russian occupation of Afghanistan. Winning of this hockey game had taken on a meaning of more than one team defeating another in an athletic event.

A talented young violinist, who had worked hard and practiced long hours, was extremely depressed and ready to quit playing the violin when another violinist was chosen to be solo violinist of a famous orchestra. This violinist's whole life revolved around being the best, the number one violinist.

Winning--being the best team, the best lawyer, the best cook, the smartest student, or the most powerful nation--is rapidly becoming the only measure of a person's or a nation's success and self-worth. It has become a valued commodity in our culture. All of us want to be successful in what we do and to be praised and appreciated for our efforts. Since not many ways have been provided for us to receive the recognition we need, winning has become the primary means for getting praise and attention. For example, winners in a softball game receive lots of attention from the spectators. There's always lots of smiling and congratulating. The losers, on the other hand, are either ignored or told to have better luck next time. A salesperson who sells the most cars in a year gets a special plaque and recognition, while other salespeople, who also sell lots of cars in doing their best, might not even get a pat on the back for their efforts.

When winning or being number one is the only means by which we receive recognition and praise for our efforts, it inherits negative meaning. Pitting people against one another, or making some feel superior to others, emphasizes the end more than the means. This contradicts the Christian pattern of life.

When winning validates a player's being hit during a game, or drives a good violinist to quit, or symbolizes a nation's superiority, then Christians must stop to re-evaluate. Such attitudes toward winning destroy people and break down community and cooperation, efforts Christians are urged to build. To be determined to win at all costs--forgetting that people against whom we compete depend on self worth--to feel like an utter failure for not winning, hardly depicts the kind of stones on which the kingdom of God is built.

As Christians, we are to strive for a life or community where people affirm one another. A life or community where people cooperate with one another, sharing skills, working together. A life or community where people treat each other as equals with diverse abilities and gifts. A life or community where all support and inspire each other in achieving without comparison being primary or success dependent on another's failure.

The Twelve were reprimanded by Jesus for arguing about who would be the greatest among them. We too, as disciples, are not to worry about prestige or powerful positions. Not motivated primarily to be the greatest, the best, or number one, discipleship invites each to measure worth through service and cooperation. Neither self or the other need be demeaned or excessively valued.

Biblical concepts noted in Romans chapter 12 and in 14:19 suggest that kingdom citizens should show love, "...pursue what makes for peace and for mutual up-building." Competing only to win usually does not make for peace. It stresses defeating the opponent, and nudging the loser to harbor anger and hateful feelings. Competing only to win rarely promotes mutual up-building. For, while the winner may feel successful and good, the loser is left to feel diminished. As Christians, we are to promote unity within the body of Christ, rather than division. Winning at all costs detracts from this. It destroys the sense of cooperation and community spirit.

Winning and losing are interconnected. When one is the best, or has the most, another presumably is worse or less valued. A's, honors, and degrees often also imply F's, failures, and dropouts. Winning may mean that the end result is valued more than the joy involved or effort made.

There are at least three ways winning can mar redeemed living.

First, winning and losing can cause barriers between people. Winning entails carefulness in not helping another too much, in not sharing information which may aid the other to improve or become better skilled. We may refuse to help a friend improve her/his tennis playing lest s/he become a better player than we. In such effort to be successful and receive recognition, we may isolate ourself. Forgetting that each has different abilities needing to be measured against personal use and excellence, we may forget the biblical incentive of serving wholeness for both the self and other.

Secondly, winning can pit people against each other, causing some to think they are better than others. One beats another out of first chair in the orchestra, or wins first place in the cooking contest, or receives a higher score on the history exam. When we consider ourself superior to others, we often put them down or "step on them." When people take a superior attitude towards us--because they become a nursing supervisor over us, or because their baseball team beat ours--we may begin to feel anger or jealousy. Perhaps a low self-image surfaces to deny achievements we made previously, or our good effort given to tasks.

When we are pitted against others, the ability to rejoice with and support them is minimized. When we are pitted against others, we become unable to live at peace. We neither love others fully or do our best.

Perhaps we didn't get first place at the science fair. But considering that last year we didn't even get to enter, our efforts show improvement. Perhaps we didn't place first in the long distance run. But we reduced our timing significantly. Shouldn't that be reward in itself? Rather than pitting ourself against another, our measure of worth can be weighed within ourself.

The third way winning sometimes works against redeemed living occurs when the desire to win prevents us from seeing what happens to the loser. Winning often gives the winner power over the loser. It can cause us to ignore the humanness of all who have entered the competition. Our winning can cause feelings of hopelessness, inadequacy, and low self-esteem to emerge in the loser. This depicts destruction rather than construction.

Since winning can create barriers between people or pit people against each other or prevent us from seeing the loser as a person of worth and a friend, what must we do to redeem winning? What must we do to foster worth for all? To measure successes without inhibiting progress for any?

Alternatives to competing just to win do exist. Ways we as individuals and as a community can go beyond the winning at all costs attitude. Ways we can develop a new sense of measuring success which are suited to kingdom citizens. Parents and teachers play key roles in training children to define success and worth in new ways. Professional and non-professional workers can create new attitudes on the job. Churches can sponsor softball or volleyball teams which concentrate on good play and improved skills. Attitudes of cooperation and mutual up-building can be promoted.

I suggest three alternatives which move us beyond winning alone, which give us other ways of measuring success. First, compete with a standard for improving personal skill rather than comparing other people's skills. For instance: a runner can focus on the clock rather than an- other runner; a tennis player can attend to improving his/her serve or coordination; a musician can master a very difficult piece of music.

Jim Ryun, the well-known long-distance runner, used the previous world record for running the mile as a standard against which he measured his own progress. After consciously deciding to break the record, he con- centrated on his goal and succeeded. But he did not run those thousands of miles in order to glorify himself. "It is enough of a reward to be satisfied within." Jim treated his competitors as friends. Not wishing to psych anyone out, he respected others. Personally motivated to "beat" the objective time clock, Jim pursued his own excellence, the outer limits of his own abilities. His prime measurement was not other people.

A second alternative for reshaping winning comes from attitudes that stress friendship and the joy of learning rather than final rank. For ex- ample, a church softball team could set these goals: everyone will par- ticipate in each game; everyone's batting, catching and game sense will improve by the end of the season. To accomplish these goals, games not won by the standard of final score may be "won" according to different criteria.

When friendship and learning mean more than being the "number one worker," co-workers can be praised for improved production, or creative systems, rather than competition. Cooperation and co-education better reflect God's pattern. Divine design credits means as well as end.

Finding new activities, or resurrecting former ones which foster support and care is a third alternative. An orchestra composed of musi- cians who cooperate provides better music than one where instrumentalists bitterly compete. Cooperative games offer fun too. Competitive games, such as musical chairs or dodge ball, leave people out and cause some to feel less skilled than others. Cooperative games, which involve all play- ers in tasks, such as building a human machine, create feelings of being needed and a sense of mutual accomplishment. At home, in the classroom, in the gym, and at work we need to recognize and affirm each person's achievement and contribution.

As Christians, our goal is to create a healthy environment for play or work. In that, all depend more on an internal sense of what is right and less on an external standard of success. "Greatness" is then measured by objective joys of learning and cooperation, or by discovering activi- ties which build and affirm each participant's effort.

We as kingdom citizens need to establish criteria that value excel- lence or success without destroying another person. Criteria that value "winning" by cooperation and by improvement.

Our endeavor will redefine greatness. It will focus on the process of achievement, on friendship and self worth for all. May each of us take seriously our Christian mandate for motivation beyond winning.

ROSIE EPP preached this sermon at Lorraine Ave. Mennonite Church, Wichita, Kansas, on August 9, 1981 while she was associate pastor there for three and a half years. She has just completed her MDiv degree work at AMBS and looks foward to co-pastoring with her husband, in a General Conference Mennonite church.

On Closing the Mouths of Lions
Dorothy Nickel Friesen

During the season of Lent, we as a congregation are focusing on repentance and penitence. A couple of weeks ago, we, together with the children, talked about specific sins which plague our lives. We put crosses made of ashes over the sins to symbolize the power of Christ to help us repent of these sins.

Today, we will focus and reflect on the theme of the call of God during Lent.

The book of Daniel contains, among other things, the very familiar story of Daniel in the lion's den. The issue for Daniel was his faithfulness. The issue was that his loyalty to God eventually conflicted with his loyalty to the King.

Reading from Daniel 6:1-9 (Jerusalem Bible)

It pleased Darius to appoint a hundred and twenty satraps over his kingdom for the various parts of the kingdom, and over them three presidents--of whom Daniel was one--to whom the satraps were to be responsible. This was to ensure that no harm should come to the king. This Daniel, by virtue of the marvelous spirit residing in him, was so evidently superior to the presidents and satraps that the king considered appointing him to rule the whole kingdom. The presidents and satraps in consequence started hunting for some affair of state by which they could discredit Daniel; but they could find nothing to his discredit, and no case of negligence; he was so punctilious that they could not find a single instance of maladministration or neglect. These men then thought, "We shall never find a way of discrediting Daniel unless we try something to do with the law of his God." The presidents and satraps then went in a body to the king. "King Darius," they said, "live for ever! We are all agreed, the presidents of the kingdom, the prefects, satraps, counselors and governors, that the king should issue a decree enforcing the following regulation: whoever within the next thirty days prays to anyone, god or man, other than to yourself, O king, is to be thrown into the lions den. O king, ratify the edict at once by signing this document, making it unalterable, as befits the law of the Medes and the Persians, which cannot be revoked." Darius accordingly signed the document embodying the edict.

Tomorrow in Wichita, Kansas, Kendal Warkentin is going to be sentenced because he refused to register according to selective service requirements. Ee is not the first to go through this process, nor will he be the last.

I think the event gives us reason to pause, to reflect, and to examine our own lives. We may not feel we have as dramatic or as public a statement to make as Kendal. But the reality of a twentieth century American citizen being prosecuted for conscience sake forces us to come to grips with our own loyalties.

Kendal stood in this sanctuary last August and gave his testimony of Christian faith. Those of us present were moved by his convictions and his desire to be a disciple of Jesus Christ. Tomorrow he may be sentenced to jail.

Just what does this have to do with the story of Daniel? As I studied and reflected on this story, I was struck by verse 5: "Since they could discover no neglect of duty or malpractice, they said, 'there will be no charge to bring against this Daniel unless we <u>find one in his religion</u>.'"

I do not mean to imply that Kendal(and others) are perfect men. However, I do find noteworthy the fact that the Jewish prime minister (Daniel), a member of a religious minority, was tested to see how true to his faith he would be. Would his actions and his words coincide? Even more so, would his actions and faith-words coincide even under threat of death?

Maybe this Old Testament story, gory and full of high drama and tension, has more to say to us than at first glance.

Reading from Daniel 6:10-24:

(Editor's note: Please read this portion, even though we are not printing it here.)

And when young men such as Kendal Warkentin, Chuck Epp, and Mark Smucker heard that the law had been signed that they should register with the government, they went to their dorm rooms.

The windows of their rooms faced east, toward Washington, D.C. They gazed out of their windows, contemplating how they would respond to the President's order. They decided to write letters telling the President they could not obey his law because God's law was higher.

Next, F.B.I. men, intent on finding those who were breaking the law, reported they had found at least three, if not 100,000, young men who had not duly registered. The President said, "Did I not sign a law? Did I not warn of punishment for those who defy the government's order?"

The F.B.I men responded, "You did. However, we have a problem. The ones who are not registering are pacifists. They are clean-cut young men, going to college. In fact, one is studying to be a preacher. They are thoughtful and intelligent. Were we supposed to catch them?"

The President became distressed. He racked his brain and tried to think of an alternative.

But he was the President. If he backed down, he would lose respect. If he did not carry out the punishment of law-breakers, the society would be damaged.

And so he ordered the young men arrested. But he also prayed and said to the young men, "Will your God save you? Do your Mennonite people believe God will save you?"

The President was troubled. He could not eat. He did not want to talk to his wife, who was very beautiful. He was perplexed with religious questions: How could it be that <u>Christian</u> young men were first to be prosecuted? How could it be that the <u>religious</u> boys were breaking the laws? Whose law was more important? Did he have faith in the God of the non-registrants? What was God's will?

Several young men went to prison. One went to work with mentally retarded adults. This was called "punishment" for breaking the law.

After one young man had been sent to jail, the President, distressed and depressed, visited him in jail. As they sat in the room reserved for thirty minute conversations, the press waited outside for a report of this most unusual visit.

Inside, the President asked, "Has your God saved you? I thought you followed a higher law, yet you sit here, in prison. Surely your God has better things to do with young men than have them be in jail."

And the young man answered,

God did not place me here; the law did. Being a disciple of Jesus requires me to love my neighbors, but it also requires me to love my enemies. That's hard to do. However, I see the selective service law as one which cooperates with a system of ideas which perpetuates the notion of enemies. Even the act of registering is an act of violence which I cannot do."

The President went away, waved aside the news reporters. He was heard to say,

My God, why must I be the one blamed for all this? Surely this is a misguided idealist who is really a Communist agent. Surely their church would not teach their young men to disobey the law just because of an interpretation of the Bible? Surely those people from the church don't really believe that.

And so, during the season of Lent that year, many people, especially some Mennonites in Kansas, were praying for courage. Many were praying for deliverance. Some were praying for mercy. All were praying for justice.

The king was overjoyed, and ordered Daniel to be released from the pit. Daniel was released from the pit, and found to be quite unhurt, because he had trusted in his God. The king sent for the men who had accused Daniel and had them thrown

into the lion pit, they, their wives and their children:
and they had not reached the floor of the pit before the lions
had seized them and crushed their bones to pieces.

  King Darius then wrote to men of all nations, peoples
and languages throughout the world, "May peace be always with
you! I decree: in every kingdom of my empire let all tremble
with fear before the God of Daniel:

  He is the living God, he endures for ever,
  his sovereignty will never be destroyed
  and his kingship never end.
  He saves, sets free, and works signs and wonders
  in the heavens and on earth;
  he has saved Daniel from the power of the lions. (Dan. 6:24-28)

And so they lived happily ever after! Trouble is, that doesn't seem
to be happening today. How come that Bible story turns out okay while
we've got people going to jail because of their religious beliefs?

But is that the point of the story? Couldn't the story be saying
something about persecution and faith? And what about courage?

Everyone must make a choice about his or her God. Everyone must face
the tests of faith. However, the only way we can have courage in the de-
cisive hours is if we've practiced some loyalty to God in smaller decisions.

Not all of us will go before judges and face prison sentences. But
some of us will.

Some of us will register for the draft. Some of us will not.

Not all of us will protest the laws of registration. But some of
us will.

During the season of Lent, especially, but throughout the year, will
we hear the call of God? And how will we respond when God asks for
loyalty?

"For God is a living God, enduring forever, rescuing, saving, per-
forming signs and wonders in the heavens and on earth. God has rescued
us from the power of the lions."

Amen.

DOROTHY NICKEL FRIESEN preached this sermon on March 6, 1983 at Rainbow
Boulevard Mennonite Church, Kansas City, Kansas. She is a senior MDiv
student at St. Paul School of Theology (Methodist), serving half-time as
pastoral intern at Rainbow Boulevard.

God's Embrace:
Bad News and Good News
Janet Umble Reedy

Several weeks ago when I spoke about my vision for our life together
at Southside, I closed with a quotation from Henri Nouwen, a Catholic
priest and psychologist. I'd like to begin with a part of that quotation
this morning.

> When we dare to care, then we discover that nothing human is
> foreign to us, but that all the hatred and love, cruelty and
> compassion, fear and joy can be found in our own hearts, and
> we can participate in the care of God who came...not to take
> away our pain, but to share it.

What do those words mean? "We can participate in the care of God who came
not to take away our pain, but to share it." That's what I'd like to
talk about this morning.

I've thought a lot about the questions of evil and suffering. At
times I've wondered, how can I worship a God who allows suffering? How
can I worship a God who doesn't prevent the murder of innocent people,
the suffering of little children, the oppression of one group by another?

One way of understanding God is that God is strong, powerful and om-
nipotent.   God can do anything God wants to. God manipulates human
beings and situations to make things come out right, or at least, to make
things come out right for those who are good, while punishing those who
are not.

But there is another way of understanding God. Through Jesus we
glimpse another reality. In Jesus, God became a vulnerable human being
who suffered intensely and took on the pain of all human suffering. In
Jesus we see that God's strength comes through God's weakness. Through
suffering and taking on human pain and sinfulness, God broke the power of
evil. That's a paradox and it's hard to get ahold of sometimes. But
one way I can understand it is with a human example.

In our culture we have a standard that men are supposed to be strong.
And being strong means they don't cry or admit to feeling pain. But some
men find that allowing themselves to cry, and acknowledging that they are
vulnerable, and owning their hurt and need for other people gives them a
different kind of strength. What may appear by some standards to be weakness is actually strength.

The familiarity of the crucifixion story dulls our perception of the
pain that Jesus suffered as a human being. There was, first of all, the
physical pain. I've tried to imagine what having nails driven through my
hands would feel like. I can hardly comprehend it.   Then, to think of
hanging for hours with all the weight of my body on those already injured
points is beyond my imagination.

Jesus experienced not only physical pain; he knew humiliation through
the contempt of the crowd. I get some understanding of that when I think
about Stephen Juday who was executed at Michigan City several years ago.
The consensus of the public was that this man did not deserve to live. The
situation must have been similar for Jesus. Even his loyal friend Peter
was ashamed to admit that he knew him. Another aspect of Jesus' pain was
the feeling that he was totally alone, that even God had abandoned him.
"My God, why have you forsaken me?" he cried.

We worship a God who suffered intensely as a human being. Our God is
not untouched by the human condition. God created the world and the human
beings in it, and God continues to care very much about what happens to us.
God created us with the freedom to make our own choices. We respond very
often by making those choices with little regard for the order that God
established, the order that would ensure wholeness and justice for everyone. The choices that we make cause a great deal of suffering, for ourselves and for each other. And those choices also cause suffering for God
who grieves to see the universe so messed up, who grieves because we are
in pain. When we suffer, God suffers too.

I'd like to give a couple of illustrations from literature. Elie
Wiesel is a Jewish writer who survived the concentration camp at Auschwitz.
He tells the story of three prisoners, two men and a young boy, who were
executed by hanging. The other prisoners were forced to watch. "Where is
God? Where is he?" Wiesel heard someone behind him ask. The adults died
quickly, but the child did not because the weight of his body was so
light.

> For more than half an hour he stayed there, struggling between
> life and death, dying in slow agony under our eyes. And we had
> to look him full in the face. He was still alive when I passed
> in front of him. His tongue was still red, his eyes not yet
> glazed. Behind me, I heard the same man asking: "Where is God
> now?" And I heard a voice within me answer him: "Where is
> He? Here He is. He is hanging here on this gallows."

Another illustration comes from Silence, a novel by a Japanese writer
Shusaku Endo. This is a story of a Portugese priest who secretly entered
Japan during a time of great persecution of Christians in the seventeenth

century. He was quickly discovered, captured and tortured. The priest
who had come with him was killed. He saw many Japanese Christians being
tortured. As he endured all this, he kept asking, "God, where are you?
Why are you letting this happen? Why are you silent?"

Over and over again, he heard only the silence of God in answer to
his questions. Until finally one evening he stood in his cell hearing
the sounds of the moaning of the other prisoners.

> Leaning his head against the wall, the priest followed his
> usual custom of thinking about that man whom he loved. Just
> as a young man might envisage the face of his intimate friend
> who is far away, the priest from long ago had the habit of
> imagining the face of Christ in his moments of solitude. Now,
> in the darkness, that face seemed close beside him. At first it
> was silent, but it pierced him with a glance that was filled
> with sorrow. And then it seemed to speak to him. "When you
> suffer, I suffer with you. To the end I am close to you."

When I am feeling hurt, when I am grieving or feeling that I can't
cope any longer, I know comfort through being hugged or being held by
another person. When words are inadequate, physical contact conveys care
and the willingness to hold my pain along with holding me. To think of
Jesus' crucifixion as God's embrace or God's hug for humanity is helpful.
God's hug says, "I love you.   I am with you. When you hurt, I hurt too."

But it says more than that, because after the crucifixion was the resurrection. Human suffering, sin and weakness are not the last words,
overwhelming as they seem sometimes. There is light in the darkness; there
is hope in despair. The overcoming power of God's love is the final word.

Sometimes there are solutions for our painful problems; sometimes
physical pain is healed. Then resurrection is very tangible. But often,
resurrection is intangible. We cannot find hope in the relief of pain. We
live with terminal or incurable illness. Political or personal conflicts
are irreconcileable. We live with the threat of nuclear war. There is
apparently no solution. But hope comes from the knowledge that suffering
and evil are not the last word. God bears the burden with us. God suffers
with us, and, through it all, God's love endures and overcomes.

As John says, "The light shines in the darkness and the darkness has
never been able to put it out." There are many little resurrections in
each person's life. Not "light at the end of the tunnel" as we were often
promised during the Vietnam War, this is light in the midst of the darkness of the tunnel. Those who are weakest and those whose pain is the most
intense, or the most hopeless, can understand this better than anyone else.
And I have learned a great deal from people in such situations.

That God is with me in suffering comes as good news and a word of comfort. God's vulnerability is the key to overcoming evil. But it comes
also as bad news because it means that suffering is real, that God does
not protect me from it or take it away. The good news and bad news of
God's embrace come to me also as a mandate. God's action in entering into
human suffering is a model for how to respond to evil. It is a call for
us to participate with God in sharing the burdens of humanity. It is a

call to join God in suffering with others.

When I think about suffering, I tend to think immediately of examples of ultimate martyrdom or sacrifice. I recall Archbishop Romero in El Salvador who could have occupied a comfortable position had he stayed with the churchly functions of leading the mass, baptizing, hearing confession. Instead, he chose to take on himself the suffering and oppression experienced by his people, putting his own safety in jeopardy by speaking, on their behalf, against violence and injustice. He became eventually enough of a threat to the authorities that he was assassinated. Or, I remember Dorothy Day, from the Catholic Worker organization, who gave up all her possessions and embraced the poverty of the homeless men and women to whom she ministered.

Some people are called to death or poverty, and maybe more of us would be if we were more open to that call. But most of us are not called to giving up our lives and all our possessions. We are called to enter fully into the lives of others, as Nouwen says, crying with those who cry, laughing with those who laugh, and being vulnerable by sharing our own painful experiences with each other so that we can learn from each other.

I'd like to give two examples of how we can share in God's suffering by entering into each other's lives. Both of these examples begin in our congregation, yet have implications far beyond it. Last Sunday afternoon a large group of people gethered together in Marcus and Dottie's living room to talk with Greg about how we might stand with him as he faces the consequences of his decision not to register for the draft. We realized that ultimately Greg must face those consequences alone. Yet, there are ways in which we can share some of that burden with him. And in doing that we are in a sense standing with all people everywhere who face punishment or severe consequences because of decisions of conscience.

Howard and Ruby have told the congregation about their desire to adopt Kim, a Vietnamese child. But in 1975 when the arrangements had all been made, Kim didn't get out of Vietnam before American forces left the country. Trying to resolve the grief over a lost child has been very painful for them. It's been hard for Ruby to understand, and harder yet to explain to others, why she feels so much pain over the loss of a child who was never hers. This has, perhaps, been more complicated than some deaths. Not knowing what happened, there has been no way for her to finish grieving. Last spring, Ruby shared her experience with a group of women who were discussing pain. One woman sized up the situation eloquently and offered Ruby perspective when she said, "You have taken on yourself the suffering of all the homeless children in the world in your love for this one child. It's no wonder that you feel such great pain." So, as any of us try in small ways to share that burden with Howard and Ruby, we too can be a part of the pain of all the homeless children in the world.

God's embrace is good news and bad news. There is no promise that our pain will go away. But in our suffering we find that God suffers too. God reaches out to us and shares our pain. We reach out to God and share God's pain. In pain there is comfort. In despair there is hope, for nothing can separate us from the love of God.

JANET UMBLE REEDY

JANET UMBLE REEDY preached this sermon at Southside Fellowship, Elkhart, Indiana in March 1983 as part of a lenten series. She is employed there one-quarter time in Gathered Ministry, attending to pastoral care within Southside's membership. Janet is also a part-time student at AMBS (Associated Mennonite Biblical Seminaries) in Elkhart.

Southside: Our Outreach Ministry
Ruby Friesen Zehr

I. OUR MANDATE

Jesus was a poor man from Galilee.

During the weeks of advent and Christmas we celebrated the birth of Jesus, the Messiah. Again this morning we sang of Jesus' birth and the advent of hope, of love, of food for the hungry. We sang of the coming of the Kingdom, brought about by Jesus, the man who spoke of love, through tears of compassion. Let me read what this man said about himself and his work, from Luke 4:14-21:

> And Jesus returned in the power of the Spirit into Galilee, and a report concerning him went out through all the surrounding country. And he taught in their synagogues, being glorified by all. And he came to Nazareth, where he had been brought up; and he went to the synagogue, as his custom was, on the sabbath day. And he stood up to read; and there was given to him the book of the prophet Isaiah. He opened the book and found the place where it was written,
>
> > The Spirit of the Lord is upon me,
> > because he has anointed me to preach good news to the poor.
> > He has sent me to proclaim release to the captives
> > and recovery of sight to the blind;
> > to set at liberty those who are oppressed,
> > to proclaim the acceptable year of the Lord.
>
> And he closed the book, and gave it back to the attendant, and sat down; and the eyes of all in the synagogue were fixed on him. And he began to say to them, "Today this scripture has been fulfilled in your hearing."

When Jesus spoke these words, some Jews knew what he meant. Some understood the new order and the leader/Messiah. Certain Old Testament texts recognized that the messianic kingdom consists of doing justice to all the poor on earth. "To know God" is a technical term meaning "to do justice, to defend the cause of the poor and needy." Many Jews knew that when the kingdom would come, it would affect the here and the now, not some far distant future. Therefore, for them to believe that the kingdom had come would have automatically elicited from them an unselfish love for all of humanity. If they believed that Jesus was the messiah with good news for the poor, they knew that he must also have bad news for the rich.

The problem with Jesus was that he was poor. The Jews had expected a different messiah--a mighty king who would sweep into the land, bringing power and wealth and glory to all. Instead, Jesus came in a stable. His sweep into Jerusalem was on a donkey. For this Jesus to say that he was the fulfillment of the messianic promise, for him to say that he had come to proclaim the year of Yahweh's favor was dangerous business.

Jesus knew that his ministry was dangerous. He knew that when people followed him, he was a threat to the existing government. He knew that the ultimate price of obedient ministry would be his death. He paid that price.

This servant Jesus is our model. Jesus' ministry shows that he is the Son of God. In the same way, our ministry is to make evident that we are the children of God or followers of Jesus in the kingdom way. To be followers in this way requires servanthood of us also, not because Jesus commands it, but because Jesus is like that.

The call to servanthood has been articulated by many people in many different ways. Taken seriously, the ultimate impact of this servanthood is always a challenge to the status quo. José Miranda in Being and the Messiah speaks about the justification for this challenge:

> Only the summons of the poor person, the widow, the alien, the crippled constitutes true otherness. Only this summons accepted and heeded makes us transcend the sameness and original solitude of the self; only in this summons do we find the transcendence in which God consists. Only this summons provides a reason for rebellion against masters and gods in charge of this world, those committed to what has been and what is.

In 1909-1910 W.E.B. Du Bois, a black educator in the south, wrote a series of prayers later published in a book called Prayers for Dark People. Here are several of the prayers:

> God, pity them that suffer with hunger and with cold--they to whom the world is but a dull and leaden toil, whose pleasures are faded memories or unreal tales of things they know not. God, pity them and us, too, if we have no sympathy for them-- if we are not willing here in these halls to dedicate our lives to the lessening of their sorrow, and the uprooting of their poverty and to the broadening of life and living for all human souls. Amen.

> Give us in our day, O God, to see the fulfillment of Thy vision of Peace. May these young people grow to despise false ideals

of conquest and empire and all the tinsel of war. May we strive
to replace force with justice and armies of murder with armies
of relief. May we believe in peace among all nations as a
practical creed and count love for our country as love and not
hate for our fellow men. Amen.

II. IMPLEMENTING THE MANDATE FOR 1982

Our congregational commitment statement begins with the affirmation of
Jesus as Lord. Our acceptance of Jesus as Lord implies that we also
accept the role of servants for ourselves. Our joint servanthood can find
many expressions. Our focus this morning is on our service outside of our
congregation, our outreach, our extended ministry.

The particular focus for today is our vision for extended ministries for 1982. Last September I shared some of my vision for the coming
year. Since then, we have done some work as a ministry group and as a
congregation so that the vision today is taking more concrete form. Part
of this vision taking shape is the budget we accepted last December. The
vision took further shape at our January congregational meeting when we
identified issues to be dealt with in 1982 and began plans to implement
ideas and programs. For this morning, I have tried to visualize our direction as well as some of the possibilities ahead of us.

Over the years, much of Southside's effort, both in terms of energy
and resources spent, has been directed toward our local community. Looking at our budget and our projected plans for 1982, we note that that will
again be our emphasis. That is quite appropriate. In a year when our
president has cut the resources of people whose existence is often already marginal, we appropriately should give generously of both our time
and our money. This we can do through Church Community Services. To become better acquainted with our community and the needs of our neighbors is
also appropriate. This we can improve with the support of Urban Ministries.
Furthering the process of reconciliation in our community is appropriate as
we support the Victim Offender Reconciliation Program. We respond appropriately as we continue to be advocates of children and families through our
support of Elkhart Day Care, Lifeline, and Mennonite Disabilities programs.

I think there are some exciting possibilities ahead for Southside.
Some of these relate to the discussion of the implications of our growth,
a discussion we did not have last fall. We anticipated that, however, referring to it as the "problem of our growth." Obviously, that is a mistake.
Or it should be. Growth should not be a problem for servants. If our witness has any validity, we should expect growth and we should rejoice in it.
So, let's continue with the possibilities, not the problems, of growth.

Here is one example of what might happen: many of our Southside families have chosen to live on the near south side of Elkhart, particularly
in the area around Roosevelt School. I think that many of you who live in
that area made a deliberate choice, and possibly some kind of commitment,
to be in that neighborhood. You knew, when you moved in, that it was a
racially changing neighborhood. You know today that it has a large tran-
scient population—in one year recently I heard a report that Roosevelt

expects a 50 percent turnover in its student enrollment during the course of a year.

Even knowing details like this, we remain surprised at the extreme poverty and need we find around us. Betty Puricelli, a seminary student who lives on Cleveland Ave., demonstrated this several years ago when she decided to visit all the people who live in a two-block area round her. Betty met the people and heard their stories. She has continued to relate to the people she met to, in varied ways, help meet needs.

Perhaps more of us could take a cue from Betty, as suggested by the Urban Ministries group. Perhaps we can establish more friendships that cut across ethnic and class lines. And when appropriate, perhaps we can invite our new friends, if not involved elsewhere, to come with us to South-side. And when Southside gets too crowded, perhaps we can divide into two partner groups, not because we disagree, but because we agree that the sharing of the kingdom dare not stop when all chairs are occupied in our chapel. Then as we relate to our neighbors as brothers and sisters in Christ, perhaps we can unite to address further injustices around us: the inequalities of the school system, the obscenity of trading food stamps for weapons of war.

I have said that directing many of our resources into our community is appropriate. However, equally appropriate is endeavor to direct our resources beyond our city, our county, our country. We can more easily focus on needs of those close to us. The hungry neighbor next door or the friend in prison--when we are aware of them--will move us to action more quickly that the refugee family in Somalia. Yet each person, whether near or far away, is a part of us. Each is our neighbor.

There are several ways in which we are addressing our more distant re-sponsibilities. The first of these is the money we have budgeted for the support of the three denominations to which we belong. Our budgeted per member giving for 1982 is an average of the per member askings of the three. This is the first time we have budgeted this much. It is an attempt to take more seriously our denominational affiliations and to share more fully in the work that they represent.

Closely related to this budget increase is a planned emphasis on global awareness. The peace committee has already planned a Christian Ed-ucation option around this topic and has been asked to follow up with some intensive input for the total congregation. We need to hear the stories of the potential refugee in Haiti, the poor school girl in Indonesia, the pol-itical prisoner in South Africa. We need to hear because we need to know them as our sisters and brothers. We need to know their hurts, to be able to respond to their needs.

III. OUR COMMITMENT

Our visions--whether for Elkhart or for someplace half way around the world--are useless without our commitment, the commitment of our time, our energy, our money, our prayers. Many of the projects we're involved in de-pend heavily on volunteers--Church Community Services, Victim Offender Rec-onciliation Program, Mennonite Disaster Service, the MCC meat canner.

Perhaps in 1982 more of us could contribute some of our time.

Allow me to comment yet on our budget. The budget we accepted in December is a pretty hefty one, and people have raised cautious questions about whether or not we can meet that budget. I think that we probably can but that it will take some serious effort on our part. In thinking about this, the stanza of a song kept running through my head. It says: "I thank Thee, Lord, that Thou hast kept the best in store; We have enough, yet not too much, to long for more; A yearning for a deeper peace not known before." The part of it that hits me most is the phrase "We have enough."

As far as I'm aware, we all do have enough. When we don't, the responsibility is ours to let somebody know that we are in need. Part of being sisters and brothers sharing responsibly for each other is our ability to receive as well as to give.

"We have enough." The words have stuck with me for several months now. I think we do have enough. We have enough for travel, for education, for recreation, for house repair. I'm not saying that we are extravagant with these. I only note that they are optional features, not the essentials of life. And when times are bad--when people in our city are hungry or without heat or warm clothing--we should be willing to give up some of our optional benefits so that a neighbor may have food to eat or fuel to heat her house.

I want to remind you again of our experience with the budget in the last two years. Each budget was increased substantially over the one preceding it and each was covered by the pledges that came in in January. I don't think that was just coincidence--I believe that God had a hand in that. I believe that when we make a mutual commitment to God and to each other, the result is not a random set of matching figures. I am not saying that because this happened for two years, it will happen again this year. Rather, I am saying that we should not underestimate the seriousness of what we are about. The budgets we accept and the pledges we make are a part of our service. God is involved in our group actions and decisions. Willard expressed this several weeks ago--God is not some distant, uninvolved being. God is here, now, with us in our faithful service.

I want to close with another prayer from Du Bois' book. Let us bow to pray:

> Let us remember those who are in the bonds of poverty who
> have neither food nor drink, the beauty of home, or the love
> of beauty. Bring us the day, O God, when the world shall no
> longer know such poverty as stunts growth and feeds crime.
> Teach us to realize that such things are not necessary to
> earth but are the result of our greed and selfishness, our
> wastefulness and willful forgetting. Amen.

RUBY FRIESEN ZEHR preached this during Southside's "commitment month"-- January, 1982. She has worked with a variety of outreach ministries and has also studied part-time at AMBS.

Mary's Magnificat and Justice
Dorothy Yoder Nyce

Luke 1:46-56

I want first to thank you for inviting me to worship with you today. This text and topic of Mary and Justice quite excite me. I have thoroughly enjoyed studying and reflecting in preparing this teaching, and I want you to know of two outstanding resources from which I have freely drawn. They are: Sidney Callahan's The Magnificat which is enhanced through photographs, and Raymond E. Brown's The Birth of the Messiah. I highly recommend them both to you. My intent is to stay fairly close to the text today, but I trust you to be alert to possible applications for our experience.

What then can we know concerning background to this canticle or song? Clearly, there is a tie in to Luke's material preceding this about Mary's going to Elizabeth's home. Elizabeth greets Mary: "Blessed (By the way, pronounce that word with one syllable only.) are you among women." Mary is blessed for her belief. Elizabeth is honored by Mary's coming, Mary the mother of their Liberator.

As for the origin of the song: there are several options. First, it may be seen as primarily a composite, or mosaic of Old Testament quotes --at least 20 verses appear in the Old Testament and apocrapha materials similar to what is gathered together here. For example, I Sam. 2:1-10. Hannah begins her song: "My heart exults in the Lord,
My strength is exalted in the Lord;
My mouth derides my enemies because I rejoice in thy salvation."
-Another option is that Luke wrote the song for Mary to say.
-Still another, less supported, suggestion is that Elizabeth might have composed the piece; the "low estate" fits her barren, older position better.
-Or perhaps this was composed by some Jewish Christians, and added into the infancy stories by Luke.
-A final option is that Mary herself is to be credited with writing the

116

song. If so, considering how young she was, she certainly would have been well informed about Israelite experience and hope. A 1912 Roman Catholic official statement does attribute the song to her. Whatever the origin, it can be examined and repeated as an expression of Mary's utter joy or thanksgiving - for her conception of the Messiah,
- for her hope in redemption through God--
redemption for the poor Israelite remnant, those she represented.
In that praise, prophetic call, and hope we may join.

The song's thought development can be examined on two levels: the general and particular. In a particular sense one woman, Mary, represents, but she also speaks for herself. She delights in knowing that God has remembered to redeem her. More generally, she speaks for the poor ones, or Anawim as they have been called.

Some explanation of these Poor Ones is useful. Originally, the term designated the physically poor--the sick, downtrodden, widows, and orphans. Zeph. 3:12 offers a wider reference: "For I will leave in the midst of you a people humble and lowly. They shall seek refuge in the name of Yahweh." The Anawim were known for their intense Temple piety. They were faithful at prayer and at sacrifice. For them, poverty was leavened by piety. They experienced communal sharing of goods. They knew persecution.

The Poor Ones are those who can not trust primarily their own might. They know helplessness, its pain and its gift.
They are those who rely ultimately on God.
They are those who regarded themselves as the remnant of Israel.

The poor ones--not the great, selfish power people--delight in promise. God's mercy toward Israel as a nation,
toward Mary as a person,
is good. To God be given ultimate praise.

The opposite of the poor ones were not simply the rich, but the proud--those self-sufficient, those showing little need of the Divine. As Hannah had spoken for the poor ones, so Mary represented them, hopeful and faithful.

Let's look more particularly at the content of the song.
First, the term magnificat. We probably think first of magnify: to enlarge or expand. Or one can associate the idea of taking in and helping another to comprehend or understand, in this case, what all God's greatness includes. This song title also means to exalt, glorify, or praise. The context of Mary's joy is God's gift of a child, her conception. Childbirth was perceived as a sign of God's kindness,
as triumph of life over death,
as a sign of the new, of beginning.
What for Mary was honor to birth was also good news for a people. They could anticipate one who would save or restore. What for Mary was a personal longing, she was able to personify for the poor ones. Her personal happiness, or being blessed, was transformed into vindicating or asserting rights for a whole people. In spite of suffering and oppression, she claimed that justice will come, that injustice will be righted.

117

For Mary to say "My soul magnifies or my spirit exults" means that her whole being <u>owns</u> the salvation to come. For the small, supposedly insignificant ones to welcome and be convinced of <u>that</u> disturbed the great, or supposedly powerful ones. Those with status--gained at the expense of others--never welcome convinced, autonomous cries from the "have nots." But that's what justice and injustice are all about. And Mary was audacious enough to know that salvation was hers,

to unapologetically claim it,

to thereby deny the control of others over her.

Mary is further described as a "lowly handmaid" or female slave,

as one who "from this day all will call blessed."

Her external condition can be described by poverty, persecution, and peasant class. From an obscure village, she and her people knew oppression. Her internal state was that of humility and willingness. She was willing to risk and comply with an Unknown future directed by a Known Presence. Of little repute, her worth was not to be measured by standard criteria. Freed from authorities named by the world, she had one Author. To that God she offered piety. She waited for God--for the God of justice, and the justice of God.

"From this day all will call me blessed." Because God has done great things for me, for women, for the poor, for all repeatedly demeaned. All will call me blessed, or fortunate, or deeply happy because they:
 - recognize my state of willingness to cooperate in the Divine plan;
 - recognize the integrative experience of birthing--
   the togetherness of emotion, will, spirit, and desire;
   the unity of will and trust--
 - recognize that I will be profoundly impacted by my child,
   that my child will be profoundly impacted by me.
   From her, the child will be prepared to go forth to revolutionary action. From him, the mother will be affirmed in
   believing in the priesthood of all believers.

All will call her blessed because of her direct access to the Almighty. Liberated from worldly authority of men and rulers, she demonstrates devotion only to the will of God. Mary's role and vocation are not dependent on her husband. Now did she need to renounce marriage to fulfill her central mission: fully redeemed, she would be fully responsible for making good news authentic, for helping it happen.

For all to call her blessed reminded the hearers of Leah's expression after birthing a child: "Happy am I. For the women will call me happy." (Gen. 30:13) Or, they might have recalled Mal. 3:12 in which the group or nation was told by God's messenger that, in the end time: "all nations will call you blessed, for you will be a land of delight..." For Mary, being blessed was a condition. Not a statement calling for worship or veneration of her, it congratulates or recognizes her state of readiness to comply with or express obedience to and faith in the God of justice. May we, in our day, bless Mary.

Concerning some of God's qualities that are focused here or God's actions that are portrayed, we start with "Holy the name."

The way by which the Divine is made known is holy. And the mercy is ever-lasting. People can start anew in hope. Qualities of mercy, power, and holiness are to be distinguished from actions identified, but they are interrelated. The qualities become the personal motivation for praise. To know God's strength or God's power is to know God's holiness or God's Otherness. With God, the ordinary and the transcendent overlap. To know God requires that one work toward justice. To hinder justice reflects on one's relationship with the Divine.

This song reveals that Mary has knowledge of God,
                    that she extends the mercy of God on to others.
The joy of birth symbolizes mercy. What a woman anticipates becomes.
Expecting is fulfilled beyond what one imagines.
Mutual dependence of being human expresses mercy.

A prime "great thing" or way in which divine power has been shown finds expression in: God routs the proud;
                    God pulls down princes while exalting the lowly;
            God fills the hungry and sends the rich away emptyhanded.
God has done this, at least Mary fully expects it to be completed. God will rout the proud of heart:
    those who ignore the point of view of others;
    those who induce in others a sense of inferiority,
        who discourage them from aspiring to all within their potential.
The proud achieve their greatest destructiveness in diminishing self-trust and self confidence in those they oppress. Hear then the triumphant anger of those suppressed: God will rout the proud and powerful.

We recall "How beautiful the feet...of those who preach the gospel." Here we see how beautiful is the anger of those who have awakened to how justice has been denied them. How beautiful when they take themselves seriously and value their own purpose. Precisely this is what Mary is doing here--assuring the people that a new order--
            coming with the birth of the Messiah within her--dawns!
For those who forced others to always be vulnerable,
    those who caused others to disrespect their own dignity,
    those who insist on controling others - a new order is coming.
                            The old order will be broken.
The new order or form of power calls for equalization. The achievement of this comes through removing "princes" of all sorts from their thrones, while exalting the lowly or those without worldly status. Removing the princes involves naming the princes' acts and calling them sin. Such acts include: persuading people that only a few must lead or control;
            distributing unfairly natural resources;
            allowing a few with property to oppress those without;
            responding in fear toward those who dissent by
                increasing control over them.
Princes make the mistake of thinking of themselves and their control as god. But only by exalting the lowly and diminishing the mighty will the whole survive. Even though the princes will assault the lowly for claiming what is theirs, God will, or has, come to the lowly's defense in send-

ing a Redeemer. That's what Mary says.

That's what Mary nudges the people to believe is true.

Further, she reminds them that God has filled the hungry and dismissed the rich emptyhanded. Her active protest against injustice expects redistribution. Like Dorothy Day and Mother Theresa, Mary, uninhibited, declares:

When the good is not experienced equitably, change becomes imperative.
When the rich fail to see need, or feel little discomfort known by others
God comes to address the situation.
"The liberation of all is necessary for the liberation of each." (Callahan) Living acceptably for God is what constitutes fullness. The hungry are those who recognize need, the need to live righteously or justly. Those God fills.

Mary's final statement celebrates the fact that God has come to help Israel. God helps or takes hold of in order to support. God is faithful, as promised--through mercy shown to ancestors past and descendents future. God's control or centrality will arise, will be present, will abide.

That's what Mary's song is all about.

That message no one can stifle for ever, much as the proud, rich princes try.

That assertive faith, passed on to the Poor Ones, is Mary's gift. It is her leadership. It is her discipleship. It is her prophecy. Of that she dare not be robbed.

But we have tried. And we have to a large extent succeeded in robbing Mary of that which she both offers and deserves. Therein we have sinned, when we ignore Mary as our model for loving mercy,

doing justice,

and walking humbly.

The Magnificat's last segment with its reference to Abraham leads me to raise a further concern. Stated simply, I believe we should compare and value similarly Abraham of the Old Testament and Mary of the New. Each was foundational. Without the faith and willing consent of each, God would have needed other plans or people. What Abraham committed himself to, Mary committed herself to.

Like Abraham (Gen. 18:3), Mary found favor with God (Lk 1:30).
Like Abraham (Gen. 12:3; 18:18; 22:18) Mary is a source of blessing for
and is blessed by all nations (Lk. 1:42, 48).
Like Abraham (Gen. 15:6) Mary is praised for her faith in the promise
that by a miracle, she would have a child (Lk. 1:45).

Just as Abraham, one man, had received the promises at the beginning on behalf of the entire nation, so one woman, Mary, received the fulfillment of those promises on behalf of the new community at the beginning of the new covenant. In crediting them comparably is a beginning step toward understanding justice.

We have been ever so ready to accept Abraham as the father of a people whom we claim as religious heritage. But we have been ever so skeptical of valuing Mary as mother of that same heritage in its new

creation, or as fulness to the old. We can value or credit Abraham without venerating or worshipping him. Why can't we respond similarly to
Mary? Granted, we repeatedly hear of the generations of Fathers--Abraham,
Isaac, Jacob, and the ten sons or tribes--while no corresponding sequence
of generations of Mary's daughters gets Sunday School drill. This follows, of course, from the fact that instead of God's people being one
nation or focused in certain descendents, the new covenant through Jesus
includes <u>all</u> peoples. Dare we think of Mary as mother, as the first
disciple of her child the Liberator?

I offer this as one response to the message of justice in the Magnificat. I wish to study and reflect on the idea further myself. At
the least, I hope we are receptive to exploring how this might offer us
all greater wholeness.

Mary's Magnificat then is:
a hymn celebrating justice and social revolution,
a hymn celebrating God's presence and process,
a hymn celebrating birth--joy in conception, reverence in anticipation,
a hymn celebrating liberation:

     liberation for those minimized (and maximized) in society;
     liberation for those marginalized by people with power to do so;
     liberation for those who believe imbalances will be upset;
     liberation for those who credit the Divine with mercy and
                                      remembering.

DOROTHY YODER NYCE gave this teaching at the Campus Cluster of Assembly
Mennonite Church, Goshen, Indiana, December 19, 1982. She will continue
to find projects like this sermon collection to bring to birth. She will
attempt to pattern Mary in addressing injustices.

A King's Story
Nancy Kerr

A children's story for Martin Luther King Day

He was not poor, not rich; but he had loving parents.
And as he grew, he was unremarkable, really...
    maybe a good boy, maybe a gifted child,
    certainly a capable public speaker.

He learned the Bible from his parents, and then from school.
As a young man he was a lover of peace and a spokesman for the oppressed.
People began to ask him for help and advice
    And always he prayed to God before he gave it.
Always he sought justice for people; always he was peaceable and non-vio-
                                                                                           lent.
The rulers began to be afraid of the power he had with common people.
    So they tried to break up the crowds that gathered around him.
He just kept on telling the powerful and the rich that God wanted justice.
Finally, he knew he would have to go to the capitol
    to speak where the power was,
    to say that the powerful couldn't forever put heavy burdens on people,
            that God would lower the mountains and raise up valleys,
            that some day, all people would eat at the same table.
Thousands of people followed him into the capitol to listen to him.
And the rulers were afraid of him and the people with him.

But things don't change overnight;
    powerful people don't like to give up privilege,
    and the poor people were disappointed that oppression remained.
Some grew impatient with his non-violent approach;
    some wanted to take what was their right by force.
Others grew suspicious of his very ability to speak or be understood
                                 by people in power;
  "He's maybe one of them," some sneered. "He's weak."
  "We need someone who can overthrow the powers and give us freedom now!"

On the night that he was killed, he had said,
  "I may not live very long, but that doesn't matter now.
  I've seen the Lord and He will finish what's started.
  I've been to the mountaintop and my eyes have seen the glory of
                          the coming of the Lord."

Do you know about whom I'm talking,
    why this is called "A King's Story"?
No, not Jesus. This person was killed on April 3, 1969.
        He was Dr. Martin Luther King, Jr.

Story

A LITANY OF COMMISSIONING
Written by Ann Weber and Laurie Oswald, Graduates

1. Family and Friends
2. Faculty and Staff
3. Graduates

1 & 2 You shall go out with joy!
2   We celebrate yesterday's steps and tomorrow's decisions.
3   Rooted in the past you have given us,
              we celebrate this continued journey.
1 & 2 We have walked with you
2   through accomplishments and defeats
1   lessons and discoveries
2   comprehension and bewilderment
1   through times of certainty
2   and times of chaos.
3   As we leave another familiar setting,
              we take new understanding with us.
1 & 2 You shall go out with joy!
1   And be led forth with peace.
3   We will follow the way of peace
              knowing that our futures will not be tension-free.
              Still, we commit ourselves to reconciliation:
1   Reconciling with our faith this nuclear age
              and demands of powers that be.
2   Reconciling our affluence with the needs of a hungry world,
              and breaking free from stereotyped relationships.
3   We came to Goshen not to escape from the world,
              but to better understand it.
              Now we go out.
1 & 2 You shall go out with joy!
1   And be led forth with peace.
3   The mountains will burst into song.
2   Trees in the fields will clap their hands.
1   You will be surprised by joy.
3   Tall evergreens in place of gnarled bushes,
              Flowers in place of thorns.

All: All this shall be a sign to everyone we meet.
          An everlasting sign of God's faithfulness.

This litany was part of Graduation Exercises at Goshen College, Goshen,
Indiana, on April 17, 1983.

When Grandpa and Grandma Crossed the Jordan River
Emma Richards

Our meditation this morning is in a slightly different form. The theme is passing faith from one generation to the next. Hear the words of scripture as they are found in Joshua 4:19-24:

> The people came up out of the Jordan on the tenth day of
> the first month and they encamped in Gilgal, on the east
> border of Jericho. And those twelve stones which they took
> out of the Jordan, Joshua set up at Gilgal.
> And he said to the people of Israel,
> "When your children ask their parents in times to come,
> What do these stones mean?' then you shall let your chil-
> dren know Israel passed over the Jordan on dry ground. For
> the Lord your God dried up the waters of the Jordan for you
> until you passed over as the Lord your God did to the Red Sea,
> when he dried it up for us when we passed over. So that all ,
> the peoples of the earth may know that the Lord is mighty,
> that you might fear and reverence the Lord your God forever."

This scripture describes for us the great way in which God led the people in days past. This morning I would like for us as a family of God's people to reflect on this great event through the perspectives of three persons who are members of one Old Testament family: through Ruth, the mother, who is the outsider; through David, her great-grandson, who is a young person and an insider; and through Jesse, David's father, Ruth's grandson, who is an old man.

Although imagination will be used to supply the conversation for this, the basic facts you can find in Ruth 1 and 2, I Chronicles 2, I Samuel 16, Psalm 114, and I Samuel 22. The setting for the story takes place in two places, at Bethlehem and the hills nearby (that's west of the Jordan River), and in Moab, on the east side of the Jordan River.

* * * * * * * * * * * * * * * *

First, Ruth, the mother of Obed, the outsider.

It's evening time at the home of Boaz, the grain farmer. The last rays
of sun have disappeared beyond the western horizon. All is still except
for the light chatter of the servants. Boaz has gone into the village
to confer with the elders at the gate, and Ruth sits alone by the garden
door, enjoying the evening breezes.

Listen as she reflects:

"That story I just told Obed! You know it leaves me both high and
low, at the same time. I don't know why! I just put Obed, our delight-
ful young son, to bed, and he said, like he often does, 'Tell me a story
about when you were a little girl!' I do that sometimes, you know. It's
good to do! But he's getting older and he's asking questions. Just how
do you tell your son that you are an outsider? Everybody, and I do mean
everybody, around here is a descendant of Abraham, the covenant-maker,
the one whose heirs are in. And me, I'm a Moabite, a descendant of Lot,
nor Abraham. I'm an outsider. Oh, someday I'll have to tell Obed, because he'll need to know. It's his right to know that his mother is a
Moabite. But now my role is to nurture and undergird him in faith, faith
in Jehovah the great God.

I learned these stories about Jehovah from Naomi. She told them to
Orpah and me when we were married to her two sons, Chilion and Mahlon,
when we lived in Moab. Now those days of widowhood are ended and I'm
married. Boaz is my husband's name; he's from the tribe of Judah.

This evening when Obed asked for a story, I said, 'How about the one
when your great-great-great-great-great-grandfather and grandmother
crossed the Jordan River?' I like that story and I enjoy telling it!
Obed's eyes got so big as I described the waters of the Jordan River,
waters that stood still. He shivered with delight when I explained how
the river bed was dry, and he beamed with pride when I elaborated on that
monument of twelve stones. It was quite a monument, you know! Of course
I get carried away a bit when I describe the stone from the tribe of Judah.
'A large boulder' I said, 'colorful and smooth.' Obed's eyes told me
that he wished he had been there to see it. I, too, wished he could
have been there, perched on the shoulder of his great-great-great-great-
great-grandmother. And then I told him why the monument was there: to
help us remember God's mighty acts and to know that God, the great Jehovah, is with us now. With that, Obed went to sleep smiling.

I feel good about that, for he is beginning to see that he is important to Jehovah and that Jehovah is important to him. My Obed will grow
up feeling like an insider. I want him to know the faith of Jehovah, not
the pagan gods I knew in my childhood. And perhaps that's why I'm a bit
sad this evening--sad for my own pagan childhood, sad for my family in
Moab. And yet how satisfied I am to be a part of the family of Judah,
to be accepted by them, and to be learning about the true God. Jehovah
is some God, you know! Just looking at those people, God knew they were
in a real predicament, and the mighty waters of the Jordan stopped
flowing!"

* * * * * * * * * * * * * * * *

Next, the story as seen through the eyes of David: the insider, the youth, and the great grandson of Ruth.

It's mid-afternoon out on the hills of Bethlehem. There is a lull as the sheep stop their grazing and David leans back against the small tamarisk tree. Listen as he reflects:

"Being the youngest kid in the family has its advantages, you know. Oh, when I'm with the others I complain alot and I remind them that they often say, 'David, do this...' or 'David, since you haven't done anything today, do this...' Seven brothers and two sisters can produce an awful lot of 'Do this's!

But being the youngest also offers some advantages for me. I get the job of shepherding the sheep. I don't want you to get the wrong impression; it's not that I don't like to work. At least I don't think so. It's just that the grain harvest is so dirty, and so noisy, and so crowded with people. I like the hillside and being alone. There is excitement out here too at times. The sheep wander off; you have to keep an eye on them. And there are wild animals; I've killed some of them. Once I killed a bear that already had a small lamb in its mouth. But most of the time sheepherding is quiet and routine. I have to keep one eye on 'the sheep, and I usually keep the other eye on the sun, so I don't eat my lunch too soon. I'm amazed at how hungry I get herding sheep! But in the meantime I play my flute and make up poems and sing and tell stories and pretend that I am someone great and married to the most beautiful woman in the world.

Yet, my father Jesse is a very ordinary person. Our family has no high social position. Sometimes I get the feeling that my parents don't think I'll amount to much, just be a herder of sheep all my life. Somehow that sort of suits me. I may never be great, but then, I do belong to the tribe of Judah. I am a descendant of Abraham with whom God made a covenant. Our history is full of great and powerful acts done by our great God, Jehovah. Nobody else has a history like ours! Sitting out here alone by the hours, I relive our history and sing about the greatness of God. For example, here is something I wrote this week:

When Israel went forth from Egypt,
the house of Jacob from a people of strange language,
Judah became his sanctuary, Israel his dominion.

The sea looked and fled; Jordan turned back;
The mountains skipped like rams, the hills like lambs.
What ails you, O sea, that you flee, O Jordan, that you turned back;
O mountains that skipped like rams, Oh hills, like lambs?

Tremble, O earth, at the presence of Jehovah,
At the presence of the God of Jacob, who turned the rock into a
pool of water, the flints into a spring of water.

I don't share these thoughts with everybody; not all appreciate them, you know. Sometimes I do wonder, did our God really have that much control over the water? Did the Red Sea really divide and the Jordan stop

127

flowing? And did all of that water really gush out of that rock? But then I hear the stories retold and I see the glory of these hills, and as I write, it all becomes mine. I do believe in the mighty God of Israel, our Jehovah.

Oh, here comes my brother Shimea! I wonder what makes him move so fast. Probably 'David, do this...' Judge Samuel is coming to our house today to make an offering of sacrifice. I suppose they need my help. Sometimes I am useful, you know. I can almost hear him, 'Stop dreaming, David! Get busy!"

And David went down the hillside that day and much to his and everyone's surprise, Samuel, the last judge in Israel, anointed David as Israel's future king.

* * * * * * * * * * * * *

The last story in this family is seen through the eyes of Jesse, father of David, grandson of Ruth. It is early morning in one of the small houses owned by the king of Moab. Jesse can't sleep, so he's sitting out by the doorway, watching the last stars fade from view as dawn comes up over the plain of Moab. Mrs. Jesse can't sleep either, so she quietly comes to sit beside him. Let's listen as Jesse talks:

"Being old is such a bag of mixed feelings and fears and blessings. It isn't at all the way I imagined it would be. I always thought we'd build a new house just for us. I assumed one of our sons would live in the big house, with the rest of our children nearby, with the grandchildren to enjoy. A scene of peace and plenty and contentment. That's what I thought: old age with the whole world slowing down so that you and I could enjoy it together.

But it sure isn't that way! Here we are, over in this foreign land, and they, the Moabites, are supposed to protect you and me. I find it humiliating! Further, Saul is out to kill David! Did you ever in all your wildest imagination think that somone would want to kill our ruddy, handsome, bright-eyed, clear-voiced child? Life seems so confusing. David is over at that cave at Adullam with most of the people from our family, and they are fearful and they are angry and they are ready to fight and destroy. Saul is proving to be such a wicked king, if you can believe the reports these days! He's been killing the priests. Where is Jehovah in all this? Is this what was intended?

You know, I had to think when I couldn't sleep this morning that my great-great-great-great-great-great-grandparents camped near this very spot before they passed over the Jordan River. I wonder what life was like back then. How disappointed they must have felt that they couldn't take their parents with them across the Jordan River, after all that wandering in the wilderness. Did those great ancestors of mine really believe that God would get them across the river, when they were sitting on this side of it? I really wonder! You know, those great stories of our family, and their faith in God, offer me help in times like this, when everything seems to be falling apart. Our children aren't living like we expected them to. But I am renewed when I remember those great stories of our family and their faith in God. That they set up those stones as a monument of faith convinces me to claim God as the great Jehovah. I don't talk about it much, but that's all I could think about all last night.

I remember my grandmother Ruth telling how they made that monument: how the stone of Judah was so large and so smooth and how it shone as gold when the sun's rays hit it. She could tell that story and the goose bumps would go up and down my back. She told it so convincingly as an old woman. I wonder how she could do it; she was a Moabite, you know. We never talked about that. Now she's gone and I have so many questions I'd like to ask her! But I can imagine her saying, 'If God could part the water of the Jordan, he'll take care of you, Jesse, even in the land of Moab!'"

And Jesse was an old man and he died and was buried with his fathers.

*   *   *   *   *   *   *   *   *   *   *   *   *

And when the children ask, "What do these stones mean?" tell them that God divided the waters of the Jordan, that they may reverence the Lord their God forever.   Amen.

EMMA RICHARDS preached this sermon story February 28, 1982 at Lombard Mennonite Church, Lombard, Illinois, where, since 1972 she has served as co-pastor with her husband Joe. Emma is the primary preacher/teacher of the word.

Mary: Blessed and Revolutionary
Mary Mae Schwartzentruber

Such a description of the woman we know as Jesus' mother is possibly surprising; at least, the "revolutionary" part might be. The small shock of the label assumes that we know the meaning of "blessed," and that "revolutionary" can't fit. Yet I wish to present the Annunciation, the Visitation, and the Magnificat, from Luke 1:26-56, as three scenes of blessing and revolution.

Perhaps the well known uses of "bless," such as the Hebrew custom of a father blessing an eldest son, and Jesus' use of "blessed" in the Beatitudes, can illustrate its meaning. When Isaac blesses Jacob, a long feud ensues, for Isaac has conveyed power on the younger son. Similarly, in the Beatitudes, divine power penetrates the lowliness of the creation as God breaks into the human experience. With such understandings, surely "blessed" and "revolutionary" stand together.

The first blessing comes in triplicate (Luke 1:28-30):

"You are favoured by God.
The Lord is with you.
You need not fear."

These gracious words are needed to prepare the unmarried woman for the final form of the blessing: "You will conceive and bear a son." (Luke 1:31) At least, that's almost the final form. And it doesn't seem out of the ordinary for a Jewish woman whose unique blessing was to bear a male child.

There are, however, several revolutionary aspects to this announcement. This is no ordinary son. His name shall be "Jehovah saves," "the Son of the Most High"! Further, this son will reign over the house of Jacob, in an endless dominion. What child is this? The mother of this child is unusually empowered.

The striking nature of the Annunciation can be better appreciated

when set alongside a parallel from the Hebrew scriptures. It is the prophet Nathan who brings a smiliar message to King David, in II Samuel 7:12.
Yahweh will establish forever the throne of David's offspring. The King's astonished reply is: "Who am I...and what is my house, that thou hast brought me thus far?" Now God's messenger brings the same astounding news of blessing to Mary, an unmarried Galilean peasant woman. That's revolutionary! The Most High was going to enter human experience through the life of Mary. Her response was to accept the costly challenge, and to believe in her own active participation in the story of God's love, as a chosen vessel of salvation.

Once again like King David, Mary accepts the word:
II Samuel 7:29 - "Now may it please thee to
bless the house of thy servant David";

Luke 1:38 - "I am the [servant] of the Lord;
let it be to me according to your word."

We who believe that the Christmas story carries the blessing of "The Lord is with you" or "God-with-us" must be prepared to become instruments of revolutionary salvation.

The second scene is that of Mary's visit to Elizabeth, Luke 1:39-45.
She is greeted with a triple blessing:
Blessed are you among women (1:42).
Blessed is the fruit of your womb (1:42).
Blessed is she who believed... (1:45).
The only other scriptural usage of "Blessed are you among women" is found in Judges 4 and 5, in the story of Jael, who tricks Sisera, the captain of the enemy army, to death at her own hands. This death brings victory to the people of Israel. Judge Deborah's celebrative song cries, "Most blessed of women be Jael," and recites the gruesome events. Thank God that this song gets turned around! Mary's blessedness among women is a work of peace. The child brings new methods of gaining victory and justice, through love and peace.

I am grateful that the second and third blessings are side by side:
"the fruit of the womb" and "believing." The power of the divine enters female experience, not only through procreation, but also through belief.
Here is a foretaste of the new order that is established in God's eternal reign.

Luke points out this re-ordering of culture once again when a woman in the crowd shouts, "Blessed is the womb that bore you and the breasts that you sucked!" Jesus replies to this woman who is accurately portraying her culture, "Blessed rather are those who hear the word of God and keep it" (11:27, 28).

Revolutionary Mary, above all women, yet standing with all women, bringing the One who would reign in peace, believed. Blessed Mary became a model of faith rather than a model of biology.

The third scene to consider is the Magnificat, Luke 1:48-55. Jahweh's obvious gifts of regard, great deeds, and mercy call out the maiden's response of exalting the Lord, rendering to God the power that is due.

Mary "magnifies" her God. I sometimes wonder if my God is too small, and whether others need a magnifying glass to see the God I trust. Not so with Hannah, whose song Mary's patterns. Her Salvation was obvious to anyone who knew her: a childless, barren, bitter, sad woman gave birth to a son! Her shouts in I Samuel 2 also exult in Jahweh. There is none like her God! Hannah and Mary serve as superb models of thanksgiving and praise.

But for each of them, that is only the beginning of their Psalm, for the God they know and trust is an upside-down God, either right-setting or upsetting, depending on whose perspective. Which of these two qualities would you ascribe to the One who scatters the proud, puts down the mighty, exalts the lowly, fills the hungry, and sends the rich away, empty? When we read the Magnificat, where do we place ourselves: with the proud, mighty, and filled? or with the lowly, poor, and hungry? Is the maiden one of those Zealots whose God will force in a new era, with a bit of help?

Clearly, Mary's song spells DOWNFALL for those without compassion. And it spells HOPE for those who have few signs in which to believe, except an upside-down God-with-us. The Interpreter's Bible suggests that this is "a salvation the great ones of the earth would not welcome. There was dynamite in it."[1] Some of this dynamite converges in Mary: an active participant in God's revolution; a model of faith, not only a model of motherhood; a hero of praise and a prophet of the just order of God's reign. Her whole being is founded on the knowledge that the Most High is at work.

In the book Call to Conversion, Jim Wallis reports that he used to ask, "How can I believe when I see how the church lives?"

"Don't look at the church. Look at Jesus," was a common reply. Wallis now sees this as one of the saddest statements in the history of the church:

> It puts Jesus on a pedestal apart from the people who
> name his name. Belief in [Jesus] becomes an abstraction
> removed from any demonstration of its meaning in the world.
> Such thinking is a denial of what is most basic to the
> gospel: incarnation.[2]

If the words of blessing and revolution don't shape up into Christian community, we can't be hearing the words of the Magnificat. We certainly aren't hearing God-with-us.

There are times in the life of the church when we have almost missed seeing the Word become Flesh. The revolutionary form of blessedness narrowly escapes us. Several articles in church publications caught my eye in this regard.

The first discusses the successful failure of missions in China:[3] God did seem to send the rich away, after they had built large institutions and imported many foreign funds. Many assumed that the abandoned, infant church had collapsed. Now, over thirty years later, we discover that God has been and is at work in China, and that the church is growing rapidly. God raises up the lowly! Robert Ramseyer, the reporter, suggests that there are two lessons to be learned from this story, both apparently radical: trust God, and trust our brothers and sisters in Christ.

The second illustration of our working, upside-down God is of the church in Russia. The author of the Sojourners article, "The Faces of Olga, Yuri, and Yolodya,"[4] suggests that while the Soviet Union is a nation where atheism is espoused, nowhere is God's presence felt more strongly.

> Christianity in Russia is incompatible with success...
> Christians in Russia focus upon the self-emptying of God,
> the divine condescension of Christ in becoming human, as
> their spiritual model. Mary...the "Birth-giver of God,"
> is a manifestation of God immanent in the humble...'It is
> difficult for us...No Bibles, no churches--but we survive,'
> says Yuri.

Third, a Gospel Herald article on Thanksgiving[5] raises the issue of that in which our "blessedness" consists. The first Thanksgiving was not a celebration of abundance, but rather a celebration of the mere survival of only four women and eleven men, out of 24 families, after the first hard North American winter. Two Indians, slaves escaped from the British, appeared from nowhere, and showed the Pilgrims how to plant crops. The power and the gift here lay, not in prosperity, but in the equality and mutuality of two races who depended on each other for survival. Perhaps our revolutionary response at this time in the history of North America would be to return the great favour by reaching out to our Native Peoples in equality and mutuality.

These illustrations, from Hannah, to Mary, to the Christians in the East, are moving and humbling. May they show us what we are to become, only through God's overturning touch.

---

[1]G. A. Buttrick, ed., The Interpreter's Bible, Vol. VIII, (Abingdon, New York, 1952), p. 42

[2]Jim Wallis, Call to Conversion, (Harper and Row, San Francisco, 1981), p. 108.

[3]Robert L. Ramseyer, "Why Did We Not Trust China Missions," The Mennonite, November 9, 1982, p. 530 ff.

[4]"The Faces of Olga, Yuri, and Yolodya," Sojourners, November 1982, p. 14 ff.

[5]J. C. Shenk, "The American Thanksgiving Story," Gospel Herald, November 16, 1982, p. 777 ff.

MARY MAE SCHWARTZENTRUBER preached this sermon at Stirling Avenue Mennonite Church, Kitchener, Ontario during Advent 1982. She is on the pastoral team of that congregation, having been enriched through earlier assignments in several overseas locations.

A Jewish Man — A Samaritan Woman
Marcia A. Yoder

When two people meet, there is potential for some kind of relationship to develop. It might be a positive meeting or it might be negative.
Sending a valentine to someone tomorrow would suggest a positive relationship to that other person. There are many other ways we express our
love and care for people. We may choose to be more intimate with some
people, more casual with others, and perhaps distant with some. Or we may
choose no further relationship with others. For instance, one might pass
at least twenty different people in the supermarket, with that being the
extent of the meeting--just passing in the aisle between the cereal and the
peanut butter.

When we meet someone, I believe we do form some kind of initial impression. They may be tall or short, thin or weighty, black, white, or yellow,
clean or dirty, loud or soft spoken, happy or sad. Our impression may be
positive or negative. If we actually get to know that person, our first
impressions may change. Our feelings, ideas, and first impressions also
may not change. Further, we may not allow the other person to change. I
may see a heavyset person and think, "All fat people are jolly, therefore,
this person must be a jolly sort." But the person may actually be much
different in nature. Because of my stereotypical thinking, I may not ever
allow that person to be anything other than jolly. Such pre-conceived
notions may even become a barrier or wall between myself and that person.

Today I will focus on the meeting of two people--a Jewish man and a
Samaritan woman. As I read this narrative from the gospel of John, three
word images came to mind: walls, water, worship. These words capsulize
something of the meeting and relationship between the Jewish man and the
Samaritan woman.

Walls....There are many kinds of walls: walls built with bricks and
mortar, walls of concrete, walls of cardboard, walls of barbed wire, walls
of hedge, walls of steel, walls of animosity, walls of envy, walls of mis-

134

trust, walls of hatred, walls of prejudice. Walls are built in diverse ways. They are usually constructed through hard labor. I remember, as a child, watching my Dad build a fence. I saw the perspiration drip from his face as he dug a deep hole for a fencepost, as he stomped the soil solidly around it before stapling on the wire fencing. Perhaps you remember when the concrete was poured for the basement walls of your house. Walls may take shape quickly or over a longer period of time. Walls of mistrust may begin when one is a child and may continue as one grows older. Walls are usually intentionally built. I think Robert Frost expresses a lot when he says a wall is for "walling out" or "walling in."

For the Jews and the Samaritans there were walls of difference which had been in existence for centuries. II Kings 17:24 ff records something of the origins of this wall between Jews and Samaritans. Remember, however, that this is told from a Jewish perspective. Actually, the Jews and Samaritans held many beliefs in common. They differed on three major points: 1) the place of worship, Jerusalem or Mount Gerizim, 2) the exercise of true priesthood, 3) the appropriate attitude to the traditions of Israel and their interpretation for changing circumstances. The Jews considered the Samaritans to be an unclean people, a people contaminated by other religions. The walls grew until the Jews and Samaritans no longer spoke to each other and certainly avoided all contact with each other.

So Jesus' decision to go through instead of around Samaria is significant in this trip from Judea to Galilee. We need not wonder that the woman was surprised to find him sitting at the well in the heat of the day, when she came to draw water. They both knew the centuries old rivalry between Jews and Samaritans. Here was a Jew who dared to walk through Samaritan territory, who dared to touch Samaritan soil, who dared to break through the walls of mistrust, antagonism, and hostility which had existed for so many years. Such a radical move would have raised the eyebrows, if not the anger and animosity, of both Jews and Samaritans.

But this Jewish man further confronted the prejudice. He also dared to speak to the Samaritan woman who came to Jacob's well. She was a Samaritan. She was also a woman. Even Jewish women were second-class citizens, treated as property. Every day a Jewish man would pray, "I thank God I am not a woman." Samaritan women knew further degradation, according to the Jews. Doomed from birth, the daughters of the Samaritans were deemed unclean menstruants from their cradle, according to the Mishnah. Not only did this Jewish man break through the Jewish-Samaritan wall. He also dared to break through the stereotypes and walls between men and women. This Jewish man fully expected to meet this Samaritan woman.

This was long ago, right. We certainly do not have comparable walls today...or do we? Are there long-standing walls in our experience, walls which are as firm as stone or concrete, walls which have the brambles and thorns of centuries climbing up and over them? Consider those of us known as Mennonite. Numerous schisms and walls have divided us over the years. We all "know" that if those M.B.'s hadn't gone off the deep end in some practices...or if the M.C.'s and G.C.'s would only have seen eye to eye on issues of mission and education....Some of these walls are old. For whatever reasons, we continue to add a new brick here or a little mortar there to maintain them. Perhaps Bethlehem '83 will actually counter that trend and remove some of the differences.

Or perhaps our experience with walls is more recent. They may have been built in the last year or even the last month or week. They may be between nations or churches or individual people. What do you intend to do about the distance between yourself and that other person? Or perhaps the relationship has actually been broken and a barrier, a solid wall, has been erected. Communication has ceased. That other person may be your spouse, your child, your friend, your roommate, the teacher down the hall, the next door neighbor, a member of this church. Our tendency is to suggest that the problem is really the other person's. They laid the corner stone. I recall Jesus' saying something about casting the first stone... let's see...how did that go? Oh, yes, s/he who is without sin among you may cast the first stone.

In the narrative focused today Jesus did not talk to the woman about stones. He talked about water. He broke through the walls of silence, hostility, and mistrust by making a request: "Give me a drink." I think the approach of this Jewish man is beautiful and insightful. He said so much in that phrase, "Give me a drink." He acknowledged, first of all, that this Samaritan woman had something to offer him. He made himself open, vulnerable, and willing to hear the other. He risked opening a channel of communication. He asked for water--something which she could give, something which he needed for a hot, dusty day. Water: cool, wet, refreshing. Water: a necessity of life, H_2O, a liquid that comprises a large percentage of our physical bodies.

The Samaritan woman responds somewhat cautiously, understandably skeptical. Just in case he had forgotten, she reminded this stranger that he was a Jew, that she was a Samaritan woman. But he proved persistent. Neither of those facts would be a barrier for him. This Jewish man continued to talk about water, about living water. She reminded him that he had nothing with which to draw water, that the well was deep. She made clear that she understood the history of the Jews and Samaritans when she mentioned the well of Jacob. As a Samaritan, she claimed her "roots" in Jacob comparable to how Jews did. This man continued to talk about water, not from human origin, but water from a source beyond the usual.

Did the woman understand the difference between liquid H_2O and the Spirit of which this man, Jesus, spoke? I don't know. But she must have recognized the acceptance this man offered: compared to the alienation from women who drew their water in the morning and evening; compared to the hostility experienced with most Jews; compared to griefs and aching mistrust from men in her life, having had five husbands; compared to some measure of loneliness from ostracism within her community. This man cared. He demonstrated sensitive love. She had known cracks in relationships to other people. She had experienced fragmentation, like Death Valley itself. She longed to be included rather than excluded, to be restored and whole rather than fragmented. Trusting the stranger who trusted her to comprehend she asked for revolutionary water.

The Jewish man knew of her needs and her capabilities. He knew about her mrariages. He knew she was a Samaritan. He knew she was a woman. He knew she was intelligent. Through a theological discussion on worship he came to the point of identifying himself to her. He actually told her who he was! He had not done that with anyone else before. He offered her living water, spirit that would quench the thirst within her.

That they discussed worship is significant not only because that was a point of contention. Through worship of Yahweh alone, through worship of the One who created us, walls and barriers can be broken. As we recognize that God intended our diversity, walls can begin to crumble. We can see ourselves as human beings created in the image of God, as brothers and sisters. To worship our Creator and value creative goodness calls for us to demolish walls. Otherwise, worship is not authentic. Worship of our Creator and Redeemer insists that we work at reconciliation, reconciling racial, sexual, cultural, or social barriers. Walls dividing Samaritans and Jews, M.B.'s and G.C.'s, blacks and whites, poor and wealthy, women and men, married and single, husband and wife can no longer exist. Worship involves meeting God and meeting each other.

In worship we acknowledge Jesus as the Christ, the Anointed One, the Messiah. In Jesus there is neither Jew nor Greek, slave nor free, male nor female. In Christ we are one. Walls which take shape through fear and personal insecurities, through the unknown, through judgmental atti-tudes, through Borscht or shoofly pie, through dimensions of sex, all will need to go. And then, like the Samaritan woman who met this Jewish men, we can leave our water jar, or immediate tasks, to go and tell our neighbors: Come! Meet the One who restores.

Learn of water eternal.

MARCIA A. YODER preached this sermon at Hively Avenue Mennonite Church in Elkhart, Indiana on February 13, 1983, which was Race Relations Sunday. She is pastor of that congregation.

The Unreported Account
June Alliman Yoder

(Sapphira appears wearing a business suit, perhaps with a small fur and a
hat, and carrying an attache case.)

Good morning. I am delighted to see so many of you here this morning.
I am delighted that you will have the opportunity to hear me speak. Many
of you know how fortunate you are to have me as your guest here today.
My name is Sapphira, and my husband is Ananias.

Down through the centuries, we have really gotten a rotten deal.
Everyone thinks we are such an ungodly pair--I mean no one names their
twins Ananias and Sapphira. Saphire is as close as anyone is willing to
get to the name Sapphira.

Well, here I am and there you are. Finally I've got my chance to tell
my side of the story. I'll be right up front with you. I'm not happy
about what happened to us, nor am I happy about the kind of press we got.

It seems to me that too often people think we were some kind of idiots
or something. One of the reasons I am so pleased to talk to you this
morning is that I honestly believe that Mennonite church people could
probably understand my feelings very readily.

When Ananias and I were first married, we started a little feed company. (We called it A & S Feeds.) We met in college. I was studying business and Ananias was finishing a degree in animal nutrition. So the feed
business seemed like a natural route for us to go. We worked hard. I
mean really hard.

For a long time it was just the two of us in the business. Then we
had good fortune--some say we got lucky--but if you're doing the work,
lucky doesn't feel grateful enough. Anyway, Ananias discovered a line of
chicken feed that just blew the top off the entire egg production industry.
And it really changed things for us, too. Ananias was busy with expanding
facilities as well as the production end of things to meet the new

"chicken challenge." (That's what we called it.) My part was to hire staff, develop a marketing strategy, and oversee the fiscal matters of a seam-bursting organization.

That was fun. It was hard work, but it was fun. <u>Together</u> Ananias and I built that corporation. Most of you are not old enough to understand the great joy of seeing your work take root and grow and flourish. But it is a great joy. We worked hard; we had a great product, to be sure. But we were also good and everyone knew it.

When I say we were good, I mean at the feed business. I don't want to appear arrogant. I'm sure we must have had our faults. And there were times when we just couldn't give certain farmers any more credit even though we knew they needed it. But I suppose that kind of solid and gutsy decision-making was part of what made us so valuable to our community.

I suppose I should get someone else to say how important we were in the community. But I assume you will understand if I just go ahead. And it really is important for you to know, if you are going to fully compre-hend what happened to us.

After Ananias was elected to the Feed Nutritionists Hall of Fame, and I was invited to the White House to meet with the President's Advisory on Women in Business, we had so many more opportunities for service. I was named treasurer of our conference WMSC. Ananias was the regional Mennonite Disaster Service coordinator. We often thought that we'd like to have been able to go on more MDS assignments, but we know that they also serve who make it possible for others to go.

And our children have always been a real source of pride for us. All three graduated from college. Judy got her Ph.D. and is now teaching at Goshen College, but the other two have good paying jobs.

With all our wealth and power comes a lot of respect, but obligation and responsibility as well. We built a nice big house out in the or-chard so we could entertain more graciously. (I believe we honor our guests by giving them our best.)

But the responsibilities are greater than that. People seek your ad-vice about many things. And when you are rich and influential, people ask you to be on boards and committees. Ananias and I always took that fairly seriously. But with those pressures, we really needed the vacations to Alcapolco, and the trip to the Bahamas was really great, and the ski break at Aspen was so refreshing. Yes, a time to refresh for greater service. And, you know, even in situations like that, there are opportunities for service. We often left an extra dollar or two for the hotel maid or the taxi drivers.

Then this church crisis came up. Ananias and I had been associated with the Christians ever since one of the salesmen had invited us to a prayer breakfast. So we did consider ourselves fully involved, practic-ing, giving, faithful disciples. And when the decision came up about form-ing a church, we voted yes. (There were three no votes, but since it was a secret ballot, I have no idea who voted no.)

Now allow me to refresh your memory. This church we organized was the first church there was--ever! It wasn't first Mennonite or first

Presbyterian, or first church of Goshen, or first church of Kokomo--No!
It was the first church ever. So we were really pleased--nearly proud--to
be what you call charter members. It was an honor we felt. And we whole-
heartedly endorsed the constitution that the committee proposed, including
the article about: "all that we have is a gift from God and it is to be
freely shared for the support of the family of believers." Or at least
that's how I remember that it read.

Yes, yes, I know Jesus preached about riches and possessions being a
stumbling block to eternal life. But we weren't like the rich young, or
the people who couldn't follow Jesus because they had to bury their parents
and all that. We did follow Jesus. You heard me...we were pillars, if you
please.

The trouble all started when Ananias and I decided it would be fun to
get out from under some of the responsibilities and sell the business and
the house and go into VS for awhile. So we did. We had sale. You are too
young to know, but those are tough times. It is like closing a very big
chapter in your life. You stand there on sale day and watch everything
fall away from you. It is tough. But we had new experiences ahead and we
were excited about that.

Anyway, we liquidated everything but our van, and made plans, as was
the custom in our church, to give the money from our property to the elders for use as they saw need among the members. It was a worthy idea. We
weren't against it. So let me tell you what we decided to do and why.

This church was the first--ever. And though we believed in Jesus
without a doubt, who was to know if this "church" organization was going to
fly? We had been very astute money managers. On these matters we knew
more than Peter--or the entire church council, for that matter. They were
good people--don't get me wrong, but certainly not acquainted with big
money, high finance, or major investments.

So Ananias and I had a long heart to heart talk. We went out to
Dandino's for dinner and we talked it through. The entire estate sold for
$635,000. Why don't we give $600,000 to the church and put the other
$35,000 in the Keoph plan, I suggested. Then, if this church should fold
up, we will have some retirement resources and not have to be dependent on
the girls.

I had taken a continuing education course called "Investment Strategy
During Inflationary Times," and the one idea that was stressed over and over
again was, don't put all your eggs in one basket. (That particular expression always amused Ananias.) So we agreed. We would give $600,000. It
would be a large gift, a generous percentage--and certainly something that
the Lord could bless and use for caring for widows and orphans in our town.

Now the question was--how do we tell Peter and the rest that we don't
have confidence in them? It just didn't seem worth hurting their feelings.
We'd just say, "$600,000 is what we got, and $600,000 is what we brought."
It wasn't quite 100 percent honest, but the intention was good, and we had
worked this way in our business and community responsibilities. We give
people our best judgment even if they don't know how good it is for them.

So we took in the money. Peter asked me if we had received $600,000 for our property. I said, "Yes."

(Sapphira falls abruptly to the floor. She lies there unmoving until a stretcher is called for and the ushers come in with a stretcher and carry her out.)

Concluding prayer:

Dear God. We can understand that you must take seriously those who would undermine your church from within. We learn that you do not trifle truth....There is no half-way mark. We stand, all of us, absolutely transparent before you. We know we must be for you, or against you; that there is no category called "sort of."

Speak to us this morning, God. The struggle is real for us, too. But we commit ourselves, our whole selves, to lives of integrity, to your living service.

With love, Amen.

JUNE ALLIMAN YODER gave this chapel address during Spiritual Life Week, October 1981, at Goshen College. She is an adjunct faculty member at AMBS in the areas of communication and preaching. She also does free lance work in public speaking, dramatic interpretation, and play directing.

Easter Reflection
Mary Beth Berkshire Stueben

This very morning Jesus has risen from the dead!

I just found it out. And I had to come share the news with you, to join with you in rejoicing. With the events of the last few days, we've all been a bit confused. We have mourned for his tragic death. But we've also been forced to realize just what an impact Jesus has had on us--truly none of our lives will ever be the same again.

This resureection has some people all shook up. They not only didn't expect it; they can't believe it. But I wasn't surprised. Since I first met him, I knew that his was the power of life.

Let me share the story of my life with you. Of those who will eventually write out accounts of Jesus' life, only the physician Luke shows interest in the tale of my meeting Jesus and what it meant in my life. (Even he has problems remembering my name. To him, I was simply a 'woman of sin' who met Jesus while he ministered in the area about Capernaum.)

My life had been neither easy nor happy. I did not have the benefit of being born into a secure, socially prominent family. I was one who was always a bit on the fringes. My parents were modest tenant farmers, who both died when I was fairly young. A distant cousin took charge of settling family affairs and married me off to an older merchant who wished to build up heirs for himself. Because I produced only daughters, I was cast off by my husband. I had failed to perform my duties as a wife. My children were placed into positions of service. Their labors were hard and they were young and frail. So they did not long survive.

As I had mourned the loss of my parents, so too I cried for the loss of my children. Following the custom of our time, I gathered my tears into a vial, a ceremonial cup that I carried with me. With this sign of personal mourning, I declared to the world the depths of my sorrow.

As you might expect, my social status was not improved by my husband's divorcing me. My future course was predictably downhill. One man treated me well, promising to care for me always, but then he died. From this tragedy too, the tears that I wept were carefully saved, stored, and carried in my vial.

For the most part, I was shunned by an 'upright' society. For that, a few more tears were shed. Most of my income came from the one task I was still considered suited to perform: the task of a professional mourner. (I certainly knew the meaning of sorrow.) A family's loss could be judged by the number of mourners following the funeral procession. To have many people to weep and lament while carrying the family's large, ornate tear vials added to their pride, to the stature of their beloved dead one. (The fact that everyone knew the mourners were hired made no difference. That a family would spend so much money for a procession was seen as evidence of true devotion.)

A life of poverty is not an easy one. Some deeds that ensure survival leave one without pride. So it was that I became an outcast, of sorts, in the community: a "known sinner." I had no family, no loved ones, and no place within the religious community. Each day, as I went through the streets, I clasped to my breasts my precious vial: all the sorrows of my life enfolded in my arms.

At this time in my life, I met Jesus.

He and his disciples had been off on a spiritual retreat on a nearby mountaintop. With that completed, Jesus came down to the plain below and spoke. There were huge crowds. People came from all over Judea, from as far south as Jerusalem, and from the north as far as Tyre and Sidon. There were huge crowds, and I among them.

The words that he spoke electrified us all. They smote our conscience, showed us new direction for our lives, cursed our evil ways, and offered us blessings. To the poor and to the ones in mourning, he offered blessing. He spoke of loving enemies, of pardoning and finding pardon. He spoke out against the blindness which sets us against each other, and of the need to lay the foundations of our lives on sturdy rock.

I was so stunned. I had to know more, so I followed him afterward. But I dared not speak to him, feeling the weight of my own guilt and pain.

Then, on his way back to Capernaum, Jesus met a Roman centurion. (I may have been an outcast among the Jews, but I was at least a Jew!) Here was one who was not Jewish at all. Instead, he was one of the oppressors of our people. Yet, for the faith and the confidence this man expressed in Jesus' authority, Jesus commended him and healed his servant.

Further along the way, he met a poor widow who was burying her only child. Jesus restored that son to life. Here indeed was one with both power of forgiveness and the power of life itself!

The crowds separated me from him, so I could not get close to him. But I learned where he was to dine that night--at the home of a socially prominent religious man.

With all the joy and hope and confusion of my life, I ran to the house, not knowing what I would do when I arrived. They were reclining at the table. I could tell he was tired from a long day, and his feet were still covered with dust from his long walk. His notable host had not even given this One the courtesy of water to clean his feet.

I rushed in, and knelt by his couch. His host recognized me and sneered at me. Then I wept. I didn't know what to <u>say</u>, or how to <u>explain</u>, or what to <u>ask</u>. (Besides, I was angry at his discourteous host...for I <u>loved</u> this man and his wonderful words of God. He deserved kindness!) Without thinking through details, I held out my vial. Then I tipped out those precious tears that I had so carefully saved and held and carried with me. I poured out onto his feet all the <u>pain</u> and <u>loss</u> and <u>shame</u> of my life: the tears of all the suffering from my unhappy life. And as they cleansed his feet, they also cleansed my heart. With my long, thick hair I dried his feet. And in my joy I kissed them and kissed them. With a flask of perfume I anointed them...

From these gestures he knew! Without any words from me, he knew. When his host chided him, pronouncing my shame, Jesus defended me. Before this man of the church, he pronounced my forgiveness. He commended my faith. He bade me peace.

In the months since then, my life has not been the same. I no longer am involved with funerals. I neither carry my tear vial, nor count and save my tears. For, I no longer live in mourning. The power of life conquered the power of death--and I was born anew.

And so I tell you, <u>I</u> was not surprised to hear this joyous news of Jesus' resurrection. For, truly, His is the power of <u>life</u>. I join with you to celebrate this day. Let us sing for joy!

MARY BETH BERKSHIRE STUEBEN gave this Easter sunrise meditation on April 3, 1983 for the Hively Avenue congregation, Elkhart, Indiana. She is current-ly a student at AMBS, having participated in the Jerusalem Study Semester last fall.

Walking the Emmaus Road
Joyce M. Shutt

Twenty two years ago, my father had surgery for cancer of the colon. The night before his surgery, he called us all together, talked with us and told us what he wanted done if he did not survive.

I've come to look back on that evening as one of the "high points" in my relationship with my parents. Dad's quiet acceptance of death, his lack of fear, his faith in God, his being at peace with himself and the life he'd lived with all its successes and failures struck a deep cord within me. Never again would I fear dying as I had before, for his modeling showed me something about what it means to live.

That evening in the hospital room, Dad asked that we read the Emmaus Road story at his funeral. When the time comes, we will. Yet somehow it seems equally appropriate to chose that as the text for this meditation, as we celebrate the 50th wedding anniversary of Ruth and Howard Musselman. Dad envisioned his funeral as a celebration, an affirmation of faith. But what else is a 50th wedding anniversary but a celebration, an affirmation of faith? For my parents, like all who weather 50 years of married life did not do it without many storms and droughts of the spirit. To have made it this far and this long is indeed cause to celebrate!

The Emmaus Road story is a beautiful paradigm of life for all of us. Most of the time, we are like Cleopas and his friend who get too close to their own experiences and feelings to be able to understand what is happening to them and around them. They, like us, needed someone to come along and to explain what was really going on, someone from the outside who could help them look through different eyes.

One of the greatest tragedies of life is that once we've lived with someone for a period of time, we assume that we know them, so we put them in neat little boxes, and act and react toward them in preconceived ways, thus refusing to allow others to show us who they really are. It also prevents us from discovering new and exciting facets of the other's personality. One of my husband Earl's little witticisms is "To assume is to make an ass out of you and me." How true that is when people and relationships are involved.

Living is a continuous experience in death and resurrection. As experiences impinge on us, the person we are is changed. A new me emerges, only to change and reshape. Our modern social patterns often make that natural sequence of death and resurrection difficult. We no longer allow each other the time that is often required to experience rebirth (or change). When the hard times come—and they are inevitable—we are encouraged to avoid confronting ourselves and the real issues. Instead, we are pushed to, or conclude that the only manageable option is, move on to new friends, new marital partners, new jobs, new churches, new homes....

A 50th wedding anniversary, however, clarifies that constancy and resolution within is an alternative. It can model vibrant, fulfilled living. A 50th wedding anniversary reminds us that along with the pain that is inevitable through remaining married to one person, living in one place, working in one major job, there are joys and rewards which far exceed the periods of emptiness and hurt.

In the 43 years that I've known my parents, there have been many ups and downs. I can recall violent arguments between them. I can recall days when they barely spoke to each other, days when the tension was so thick one became almost paralysed from it. Also, I recall days of infinite tenderness, of life-enriching love, of laughter, of quiet serenity, of fun and relaxation, challenge and affirmation. Like the night (in the hospital) Dad spoke of the possibility of his impending death and the modeling that offered. I remember, during my teen years at home, the difficulties Dad and Mother encountered in their own mid-life crises. What a pleasure now to see them enjoying each other, being affectionate, doing tasks together, reveling in shared activities, many of them newly discovered. Those memories—of the bad times, the pain and struggle, the anger hatred, violence, and despair—have known redemption through resurrection into renewed commitment and love.

Those memories, more than anything else, have kept me going during the long, dark nights of my own marriage and family trauma. For, my parents modeled in the most dramatic way—through their own experience—that there are solid reasons for not separating when love, hope, passion, and dreams seem to be gone. They modeled that commitment to a partner does not need to correspond with devaluing self, giving up personal interests, or becoming less than one can become. In their own way, they have been the familiar stranger (unrecognized until later) walking the Emmaus Road with me (and how many others?) explaining the mysteries of life, marriage, fidelity, commitment, friendship through the lens of their own experience.

Having said all this, I realize that I've probably caused some of you pain. Your lives may not have followed the pattern Dad and Mother chose. Your circumstances likely differed. Divorce met with more difficulty in my parent's day. Some of the stigma connected with separation

146

and divorce has been relieved today. Choices have been made which force some of you to face life differently. Yet, the values of which I speak are still applicable to you. Your own experience, your own challenges, like theirs and mine, can contain comparable impetus for renewal and growth, for resurrection. When we are willing to learn from our stories instead of being ashamed of them, we are freed to confront ourselves, with all our strengths and weaknesses, and to love in God's open future.

Several months ago we took a Sunday morning to talk with each other about families and family life. That morning, instead of a sermon, we talked with each other openly and candidly, sharing our hurts, fears, and needs. One of the most poignant things said that morning was Kris's verbalizing for our youth, "With all the marriage break-ups, I'm almost afraid to risk loving and getting married."

The realization from her plea, or fear, is that love involves risk. There can be no loving without risking, for that is the nature of love. Reaching outside oneself to emphasize another's importance makes us vulnerable. It frequently brings pain and suffering. But that need not immobilize us. Around us are stories that prove durability. Couples have found ways within their own marriages to adapt, adjust, model, shape, and emerge. Look to them to model longevity in relationships. Then discover your own pattern, a way that suits you and your partner. "'Til death do us part" is an awesome commitment. But it is possible. The proof lies in those who, in spite of struggle, pain, and hard work, have achieved that goal.

On the way to the airport on Wednesday, Carolyn and I talked about all sorts of things, including 50th wedding anniversaries. Among other tidbits of wisdom, she said, "A 50th wedding anniversary to me is like a piece of driftwood or a stone along a beach. The rubbing and buffeting of the waves, the tumbling and grinding of the stones, the pounding of the storms...don't destroy the driftwood or stone. Instead, they smooth, polish, reshape, and mold the piece into a harmonious, graceful thing of beauty."

Along the Emmaus Road the stranger spoke to Cleopas and his friend of the mystery of life, of death and resurrection, of hope and promise in spite of fear and pain. Death and resurrection. How often must we die? How often do we need to go through the awful pangs of giving up what we've loved and valued to reach for the unknown and new? Just as often as our hopes, dreams, aspirations, and needs interfere with the unfolding and growth of loved ones around us. As long as our insistence on one pattern prevents ourselves or others from experiencing newness and re-creation of life.

Death and resurrection. The end and the beginning. One blends into another so smoothly that knowing where one stops or begins may be difficult. But one surety remains: death and resurrection, or buffeting and reshaping, is part of God's plan for our lives. As we daily die, may we rise to celebrate and affirm the wonder of God's world and life for each of us!
    Amen.

JOYCE M. SCHUTT

JOYCE M. SCHUTT used this sermon twice. The first time it was the meditation for a special worship service to celebrate her parent's 50th wedding
anniversary. The second time it served as a memorial meditation for a
private service her congregation had two weeks after her father was killed
in an automobile accident. Joyce is pastor of the Fairfield Mennonite
Church, Fairfield, Pennsylvania.

Growing in Grace, Giving, and Gumption
Marilyn Miller

At the age of 85, E. Stanley Jones was speaking at a seminary. He had written 25 books and was still going strong--travelling, speaking and writing. He told his seminary audience, "It's fun being a Christian at 25, 35, 45. It's fun being a Christian at 85 and getting funnier all the time."

When asked the secret of his lifelong zest, Jones gave primary credit to grace and gumption. Grace and gumption are very important elements in my life, also. To those two words I want to add another word--giving.

I would like to share with you how I have experienced these words in my life, but first let's look at a woman in the gospels whose story showed GRACE, GIVING, and GUMPTION. Then, I invite you to think about your stories and the meaning of these words for your lives.

Our Bible story found in Luke 7:36-50 is a beautiful story. Jesus is reclining at a dinner table when a woman appears. She is weeping and her tears fall on the feet of Jesus. She takes her long hair and wipes those tears. Then she kisses his feet and pours very expensive perfume on them.

Simon, the Pharisee, who had invited Jesus to dinner, is aghast. He says to himself, "If this man were a prophet, he would know what sort of person touched him." Jesus shares a parable with Simon to help Simon see that the person who has been forgiven much, the person who has truly experienced grace, loves much and gives much.

Then Jesus says to the woman, "Your sins are forgiven....Your faith has saved you...go in peace." And, no doubt, she went in peace. For she had been accepted as she was. She had experienced grace.

Grace--unmerited, undeserved love and mercy. Paul Tillich describes grace this way:

Grace strikes us when our disgust for our own being...our
weakness, our hostility, and our lack of direction have become

149

intolerable to us. Sometimes, at that moment, a wave of
light breaks into our darkness and it is as though a voice
were saying, "You are accepted. You are accepted, accepted
by that which is greater than you. Simply accept the fact
that you are accepted.' If that happens to us, we experience grace.

What happens when we experience grace? We feel love and want to
give. The woman in the Bible story felt love and expressed it by giving
--by pouring perfume on the feet of Jesus. Jesus said to Simon, "And so,
I tell you, her great love proves that her many sins have been forgiven;
where little has been forgiven, little love is shown." In other words,
where little grace is experienced, there is little giving from the heart.

In each of the other gospels there is a somewhat similar story of a
woman showing her love to Jesus by giving--by pouring expensive ointment
on him. Although they vary in detail, and may very well be different
incidents from the Luke account, they all display grace, giving, and gumption.

In Mark's account (14:3-9) Jesus is sitting at the table, when a woman comes in with an alabaster jar of very costly pure nard. She breaks
it and pours it over his head. And the people present criticize: "Why
this waste? This ointment might have been sold for a large sum and given
to the poor." But Jesus said, "Let her alone....She has done what she
could. She has done a beautiful thing for me."

The people who were criticizing saw only "dollar signs." But Jesus
saw beyond the ointment and money. He saw a person, a woman, giving her
love, giving herself. The perfume was a mere sign of that love, of that
self-giving.

This giving was not easy for the woman to do. In those days a proper
woman did not break up a meeting of men with her words and acts. This
woman probably knew she would be criticized and condemned but she had experienced grace, and in response she wanted to give of herself. The grace
she had received gave her the energy, the true grit, the gumption to act,
to give of herself despite the criticisms. And Jesus said, "She has done
a beautiful thing."

Put GRACE, GIVING, and GUMPTION together and it can be beautiful.

Well, that's the bible story. Now I would like to share with you
some of the ways I have experienced grace, giving, and gumption in my own
life.

First, GRACE. Grace for me is no mere theological proposition; it
is as real as hamburgers and milkshakes. I have experienced grace as an
energizing power. Often I have come to know it and experience it through
the incarnate spirit of Christ working in other people.

There is my parental family: my parents, Milo and Clara Kauffman,
and eight siblings with whom I can say anything and be anything. They
will let me know if they don't like it, but underneath their disagreement
or disappointment I feel a foundation of love that will always be there
even if it is not deserved. That's grace.

Then, there is my husband, Maurice, whose love calls out the best in me, whose love encourages me to grow, who I know stands behind me when I'm at my worst as well as when I'm at my best. I think of our three children. One evening I was very tired. I was leaving on a trip the next day and had many, many things to do first. At the evening meal I was cranky and impatient with the children. Then I went off to a meeting. I came home feeling very low, alone, and tired--knowing there was much yet to be done. When I walked in the door, I found three children vacuuming and dusting, finishing up the last of the house cleaning. I was overwhelmed. After my crankiness with them, this was so undeserved! My low, lonely feelings left and I received a new energy to go on with my work. That's grace!

I think of the Lorraine Avenue Church in Wichita, Kansas and the Arvada Mennonite Church in Colorado where Bible study groups and friends and pastors were able to share their failures and humanness with me and I with them, and where God's love, acceptance, and forgiveness became more real to me as I experienced them through other people.

I think of times when meditating on scripture and praying, or when listening to music when I felt the closeness of God and God's love for me despite my unworthiness. When I feel that grace I want to give myself back to God in love. I, like the woman in the Bible story, want to give what is uniquely me. What are the gifts that I have to give to the Lord?

When I was a child, I thought I had the gift of preaching, so I would gather my sisters and brothers and neighborhood children together and hold evangelistic services for them. When they got tired of listening, my sister, Joy, and I would move out to the hen house. We had a roost there that looked like chorus risers, so Joy would put the chickens on the risers and lead the "cackle choir" and then I would preach to those chickens. I didn't receive many "Amens" from them, but there was lots of cackling, and some bewilderment on the part of my parents who wondered about the sudden loss in egg production.

Needless to say, I had to quit preaching to the chickens, but I remember thinking, "If I were a man, I would be a preacher." In those days I didn't know of one female pastor, so I didn't dream that one day I would preach to real live people. But I did decide to marry a minister so I could do church work through him. Then my "shining knight" came riding up in his new black and white Ford, and I fell in love. He said no way did he feel called to be a minister. Well, the heart ruled over the head, and we married.

I taught school for five years while Maurice finished his degrees. Then he worked as a city planner and for nine years I stayed at home, busying myself with homemaking, three children, and various types of church activities.

One Sunday the pastor of our church, in a sermon, referred to Bro. Lawrence, a monk who practiced the presence of God among the pots and pans of a kitchen. Since I was spending a lot of time myself those days among the pots and pans, I decided to do some more reading about Bro. Lawrence. One story that I read about his life really struck me.

One winter day Bro. Lawrence went out for a walk. As he walked he
came upon a large, gnarled, barren tree. It was just an ordinary tree
and probably many people had walked right by it without a second thought.
But as Bro. Lawrence looked at the tree, he thought about how it soon would
be breaking forth with buds and then beautiful leaves and new life.
Then the revelation hit him, "If God can bring about such changes in an
ordinary tree, what could he bring about in me if I would be open?"

Bro. Lawrence opened his life to God and practiced his presence among
the pots and pans of the kitchen and his life blossomed forth like a tree
in springtime, bringing beauty and more abundant life to many people who
came to learn from him.

As Bro. Lawrence opened his life to God, so I desired to open my life
and let God work through me. I remember kneeling beside our bed one
morning years ago in Wichita, Kansas, and saying, "Lord, I give myself
completely to you. I'll go anywhere, do anything, just let me know your
will."

Well, the answer came much sooner than I expected. That evening
Maurice came home from work and the first thing he said was, "Marilyn,
how would you like to move to Denver?" Right away, I thought--my devo-
tions this morning; I said I'd go anywhere." I had experienced the grace
of God; I had given myself to God, and now I needed some gumption in order
to leave our many close relatives and friends to move to Colorado.

Gumption was needed after we moved to Arvada--gumption to drive the
busy expressways of Denver across town to a strange new Seminary where I
knew no one. Gumption to take tests and write papers while trying to
keep up a home and family.

I didn't know what my seminary training would lead to. I remember
telling my advisor, "I'm a woman, and I'm a Mennonite, and I know of no
Mennonite church in the area that hires a woman for anything except sec-
retarial or janitorial work. I doubt if I can get any kind of job in
the Mennonite church when my seminary training is done."

So I was surprised when offered an interim pastoral position at First
Mennonite Church in Denver and then doubly surprised when my own church,
Arvada Mennonite, offered me a position. Now I wish I could say to all
of you women, "Just trust God. If God is calling you to the ministry, the
doors will open for you, just like they did for me." But I can't truth-
fully say that. I know too many women who are as capable, or more capable, than I am and who have sensed God's call to the ministry and yet
have had no job offers.

I thank God that people in Arvada had open minds and open hearts to
test God's call and I pray that will happen in more of our Mennonite churches. My experience as co-pastor with Peter Ediger at Arvada Mennonite
Church has been a very rewarding growthful time. But it has not always
been easy. There have been criticisms. My mother-in-law wrote and asked,
"Isn't it unfeminine for a woman to be a pastor?"

And my very own mother came to Colorado for my ordination. In our
morning worship service we have a sharing time and she got up and held up

her Bible. She stated that she believes the Bible teaches that a woman should stay at home and be a helpmate to her husband. She said that she knows I believe differently and that I have her blessing but she did want the congregation to know where she stood. She did not want to be a hypocrite. Well, she went on and on. When she finished, the congregation gave her a big hand. All I could say was, "Mom, for a woman who doesn't believe in women preaching, you have certainly given a tremendous sermon." Although Mother and I could both laugh at this, there have been times when it has taken some gumption to face criticism and the frustrations and struggles that come with pastoring.

There are times on Saturday nights when the family is watching TV or playing a game together and I'm sitting at my typewriter wondering if the sermon is going to come together by morning and wondering why in the world I'm taking on all this work, anyway.

But usually by Sunday afternoon I know again why I am in the work I am and why all the sacrifices are worth it. Sunday morning the beautiful people in the Arvada congregation help me experience grace again, and I go away from them wanting to give even more. I spend a relaxed Sunday afternoon with family members, feeling love and grace from them. Then I want to give even more to them too.

It's kind of a cycle. I experience grace....With the grace comes an urge, or call, to give of myself. But often, to respond to the call, I must risk and sacrifice. When I have the gumption to do so, it often leads to a new grace experience....and the cycle goes on.

What about grace, giving, and gumption in your lives? How have you experienced grace in your life? Have you been feeling what God tells us over and over in scripture--that you are forgiven, loved, and accepted because you are God's child? Many of you know from experience what this means.

I remember my mother loving and caring for her youngest son, a child born with Downs Syndrome. This child would never be able to do much or be much, but he was her child and she loved him for who he was. I remember holding our first child, who was born dead. She could not respond to me. She would never do anything for me, but my love for her was great. She was part of me--my child.

And God's love is even greater than a mother's love. Listen to the words of Isaiah 49:15. "Can a woman forget the infant at her breasts or a loving mother the child of her womb? Even these forget, yet I will not forget you."

When we experience God's great love, forgiveness, acceptance, we experience grace. When we experience grace, we want to give ourselves to God's service. And we ask, "What do we have to give?" I Peter 4:10 says, "God has given each of you some special abilities; be sure to use them to help each other, passing on to others God's many kinds of blessings." (Phillips)

Each of you has something to give that no one else can give--your unique self, your attitudes, your gifts, your skills, your opportunities to reach certain people that no one else may be able to touch. God does

not want you to be like me. God does not want you to be like the woman who
poured perfume on the feet of Jesus. Our Creator wants you to be uniquely
you.

In the book Dobry Grandfather expresses the following:
Everything is different, each leaf, if you really look.
There is no leaf exactly like that one in the whole world.
Every stone is different. No other stone is exactly like
it. God loves variety....The Creator makes a beautiful thing
and nothing else in the world is exactly like it....In odd days
like these, people study how to be all alike instead of how
to be different as they really are.

To give gifts that are uniquely personal is hard for us when society
pressures us to be like everyone else. Some years ago there were some
women who felt very unfulfilled being full-time homemakers, but society
said, "You belong full-time in the home." So they stayed there.

Today there are some women who say, "I want nothing more than to stay
at home and be a creative homemaker. That's where I get my joy and fulfillment and that is where I can be creative and do the most good." Yet
some of these women tell me, "I feel guilty staying at home now that the
children are in school. People keep asking me, 'What do you do with all
your time?'"

If we let others make us feel guilty, if we listen only to others,
and not to our own inner feelings and to God, we may never develop and
give those gifts that are uniquely ours to give.

When we experience grace, and when we desire to give what is uniquely
ourselves, we often find that we must risk, and that takes gumption.   God
may call us to use our gifts in places where we will be criticized. I
talked to a woman who said that some people in her church thought she had
gifts that would make her a fine deacon, so they wanted to put her name on
the election ballot. She said, "I refused. No woman has ever been a deacon in our church, and if I ran, I would be crucified." That church was a
loser because the gifts of that very qualified woman stayed dormant, and
the woman was a loser, for her gifts can not grow if they are not exercised.

I have to wonder what the church has lost in progress and achievement
in furthering the kingdom, because of our failure to risk finding, developing, and using the gifts God has given to us.

Each of us, like the woman in the Bible story, is gifted with an alabaster jar. In it we carry a very precious perfume, our own unique personalities. We can choose to go through life carrying that precious perfume
in an unopened jar, waiting for a time when there won't be much risk in
opening it and sharing it. Or, we can choose to measure that perfume out
with a medicine dropper, little by little, sharing it only with those we
think will appreciate it. Or, we can do as the woman in the Bible story,
and pour the contents at the feet of Jesus.

If we do so, there is apt to be noise about it. Some people will say,
"Not practical....What a waste....We didn't say you could do that!....
You're wrong!"

But there will be one voice, whispering maybe, saying to those who hear, "Let her alone....She has loved much....She has done what she could ....She has done a beautiful thing for me."

MARILYN MILLER gave adaptations of this sermon in three different settings: -a Women's Missionary Organization Meeting, Buhler, Kansas, Oct. 22, 1977; -the 29th Annual Woman's Fellowship, Camp Menno Haven, Tiskilwa, Illinois, Nov. 15, 1979;- chapel:- Associated Mennonite Biblical Seminaries, Elkhart, Indiana, Nov. 9, 1982. Since 1975 Marilyn has served as co-pastor of the Arvada Mennonite Church, Arvada, Colorado; she is presently working on a Doctor of Ministry degree from San Francisco Theological Seminary.

From this Hour
Gertrude Roten

The privilege is mine to worship with you.
This is a joyous occasion, the commissioning of a dear person, Martha Smith,
to the service of this church and community.

Erland Waltner asked me to extend greetings from the Associated Mennonite
Biblical Seminaries to the Stirling Avenue Mennonite Church and to Martha
on this occasion. Millard Lind also sends personal greetings to you,
   Martha.

Such an occasion presents responsibilities for the individual and for the
   church.
Let us turn to Exodus 3 to read of the call of Moses,
and the responsibilities laid upon him and upon the Children of Israel.

Now Moses was keeping the flock of Jethro, his father-in-law,
the priest of Midian
and he led the flock to the back of the wilderness,
and he came to the mountain of God, unto Horeb.

And the angel of Jehovah appeared unto him in a flame of fire
out of the midst of a bush;
and he looked, and behold, the bush burned with fire,
and the bush was not consumed.
And Moses said, I will turn aside now,
and see this great sight, why the bush is not burned.

And when Jehovah saw that he turned aside to see,
God called unto him out of the midst of the bush, and said, Moses, Moses.
And he said, Here am I.
And he said, Draw not nigh higher: put off thy shoes from off thy feet,
for the place whereon thou standest is holy ground.

Moreover, he said, I am the God of thy father
the God of Abraham, the God of Isaac, and the God of Jacob.
And Moses hid his face: for he was afraid to look upon God.

And Jehovah said, I have surely seen the affliction of my people
that are in Egypt,
and have heard their cry by reason of their taskmasters;
for I know their sorrows,
and I am come down to deliver them out of the hand of the Egyptians
and to bring them out of the land, unto a good and large land,
unto a land flowing with milk and honey;
unto the place of the Canaanite, and the Hittite, and the Amorite, and the
Perizzite, and the Hivite, and the Jebusite.
And now, behold, the cry of the children of Israel is come unto me:
moreover I have seen the oppression wherewith the Egyptians oppress them.

Come now therefore, and I will send thee to Pharaoh,
that thou mayest bring forth my people, the children of Israel out of Egypt.

From this account, one can conclude that Moses,
wending his way homeward that night with the sheep of Jethro,
had experienced the holiness of God.

He hid his face as God made himself known to him.

Isaiah, at the time of his call, said
Woe is me! for I am undone.

The maiden from Nazareth, in the hour of her call,
experienced the holiness of God in this way,

The Holy Spirit shall come upon thee
and the power of the most high shall overshadow thee:
wherefore also the holy thing which is begotten
shall be called the Son of God.

The congregation of Israel recognized that Moses had faced
the holiness of God. They trusted him.

Moses' background training in the knowledge, and in the wealth, and the
"swing" of Egypt did not make the people leary of him.
They confided in him: there was no credibility gap: no swindling.

His life was exemplary. Aaron had the silver tongue,
but while Moses was on the mountain of God, Aaron could not lead.

They knew where Moses' tent was pitched. They knew that their day to day
behavior stood against the backdrop of God's holiness.
They knew that Moses held his own day to day behavior toward God,
toward his fellowmen, and toward all of creation, against the backdrop of
God's holiness.

What implications does this have for a congregation

which accepts a person who has experienced the holiness of God?

There is an integrity in relationships,
There is reverence for God and for God's servant, on the part of the con-
    gregation.
Idle and malicious talk is absent. Tho' the pastor may not be like the
    former pastors,
there is acceptance of the pastor's capacities.
Confession of error is made openly and freely. Hidden agenda has no place
on the part of the members in relation to the church.

There is a reverence for God and for the congregation on the part of the
    pastor.
Tho' the congregation may not be as former charges,
the pastor will not try to remold them out of character. There will be
    patience,
the careful keeping of confidence.   There will be mutual trust.
A pastor too will be open in confessing shortcomings to the congregation.

The presence of the shepherd brings quiet; the voice, the smile, the tears,
the pat on the shoulder, the handshake,
These can convey God's holiness.

From this account, one can conclude, that Moses,
wending his way homeward that night with the sheep of Jethro,
had experienced God's need of him,..."Come"...

Isaiah, at the time of his call, felt the need, through a question from God:
Whom shall I send and who will go for us?

The maiden from Nazareth learned of God's need for her through the greeting
of the angel:
Hail, thou that art highly favored, the Lord is with thee.

God's need was answered by Moses' action: he pulled up stakes.
He left behind the herd of sheep.
He said to his father-in-law:
I pray, let me go back to my kinsmen in Egypt
and see whether they are still alive.

The Children of Israel were aware that Moses felt needed by God,
They themselves began to feel that God needed them, a peculiar people,
to reveal, through them, Divine nature to humanity,
That they were a chosen people rather than a favored people.
Chosen to act: chosen to pull up stakes
Needed to move amongst the Canaanites: to act out their form of worship,
to depend upon God in warfare, to worship the one true God.
Ready to move today: ready to stay tomorrow.

What implications does this have for a congregation which accepts a person
who has experienced God's need for her or him?

The pastor translates this need into action. His or her action already
has taken shape by accepting the leadership role.
The church accepts the work at hand: The church acts with the pastor as a
need arises in the congregation, community, country, world.

God needs you: you go into action: action like the peace stand, the
    quiet in the land,
the simple life, the separate life, letting blood or chaining oneself to
the doors of the Pentagon or Ottawa, refusal to pay war taxes, disaster
    service, etc.
God needs a leader, a people; they are God's hands and feet.

This may mean for a church member to pull up stakes in the middle of life,
to change vocation, to examine motives, to become a pilgrim on earth with
no abiding city. This may mean that some teenagers will say, "Mom and Dad,
I just must to--into VS work, into giving my body for medical experimenta-
tion or wellness-control in testing, into the ministry. God is saying,
to me, Come."

From this account, one can conclude that Moses,
wending his way homeward that night with the sheep of Jethro,
had experienced God's authority.

Moses had replied to God at the burning bush,
Who am I, that I should go to Pharaoh,
that I should bring forth the Children of Israel out of Egypt?

God said, Certainly, I will be with thee.

And Moses said, Behold when I come to the Children of Israel,
and shall say unto them
The God of your fathers has sent me unto you;
and they shall say unto me, What is God's name?
what shall I say to them?

And God said unto Moses, I AM THAT I AM:
thus shalt thou say unto the Children of Israel.

Isaiah, in his hour, experienced comparable authority of God.
Then I said, here am I, send me.
Then God said, Go and tell this people...
Then I said, Lord, how long?...
Then God answered, Until cities be waste without inhabitant
and houses without people, and the land become utterly waste.

The maiden of Nazareth in her hour experienced the authority of God
in the voice of the angel:

He shall be great, and shall be called the son of the most high.
And the Lord God shall give unto him the throne of his father David,
And he shall reign over the house of Jacob forever,
and of his kingdom there shall be no end.

Moses went back at the peril of his life.
The guilt of the slain Egyptian could have continued to gnaw at him,
the fear....

He stuttered: what did this mean?

A slave psychology had penetrated deeply into Israel. It was part of him
He had identified with them. That is why he fled.   too.
Not to go into the presence of President Jimmy Carter, or Premier Pierre
    Trudeau...
No, of Pharoah.
In that hour, Moses had experienced deeply the authority of God.
And Moses took his wife and his sons, and set them upon an ass
and returned to the land of Egypt,
And Moses took the rod of God in his hand.

The Children of Israel were aware that Moses had experienced the authority
    of God.

Since the arrival of Moses, the making of bricks becomes more difficult.
The straw is taken away.
The cry goes up, how long? why?

Water turns to blood, frogs, lice, flies, cattle disease, boils, hail,
locusts, darkness: Then, there is the breakthrough,
The passing of the angel.
The last meal is eaten in haste, the unleavened bread, the unblemished lamb.
Then the cloud by day: the pillar of fire by night,
The Red Sea opens; the way is clear: Salvation History is made.

The Children of Israel felt the authority of God.
Life was never the same again.
A turning point had come, a point of reference:
When your son comes to you and asks you...tell him...I saved you
out of the land of bondage - I led you through the Red Sea.

As Moses bows to the authority of God, so do they.
Open to the dangers of the desert, to enemies,
as Moses stands still,
so they stand still, and know that Jehovah is God.

They follow in being a people apart, apartheid.
They live by the ten commandments, they build a tabernacle with no idols,
They practice the sign of the covenant given to Abraham.
They do not sacrifice children. They worship One God.

What implications does this have for a congregation which accepts a person
who has experienced the authority of God?

God's word will be taught to the young...when you sit in your house,
when you walk by the way,
when you lie down and when you rise up....

There may be suffering ahead: sacrificial giving, obedience to the call
of full-time service, making restitution with a sister or brother,
a change of life style, discernment of gifts which may be painful,
persecution and death.

This person who has experienced God's authority,
calls out with the writer of Ephesians:

For this reason,
assuming that you have heard of the stewardship of God's grace
that was given to me, how the mystery was made known to me...
which was not made known to the descendents in other generations,
Of this gospel, I was made a minister according to the gift of God's grace,
which was given me by the working of God's power,
To me, though I am the very least of all the saints, this grace was given,
to preach the unsearchable riches of Christ
And to make all people see what is the plan of the mystery
hidden for ages in God who created all things;

That through the church, the manifold wisdom of God
might now be made known, to the principalities and powers
in the heavenly places.

But grace was given to each of us
according to the measure of Christ's gift.

And those gifts were that some should be apostles, some prophets,
some evangelists, some pastors, and teachers,
for the equipment of the saints,
for the work of ministry,
for building up the body of Christ.

Grace was given to each of us...
according to the measure of Christ's gift.
To each one of us...under the authority of God.
The priesthood of the believers.

From this account, one can conclude that Moses,
wending his way homeward that night with the sheep of Jethro,
had experienced the love of God for him and God's people.

Tho' the word "love" is not mentioned at the burning bush,
God said to Moses. "I am the God of thy Father."
Concerning the Children of Israel, God said,
I know their sorrows.

Isaiah, in that hour, experienced God's love thus:
"Then flew one of the seraphim unto me,
having a live coal in hand,
having taken it with the tongs from off the altar,
and the seraph touched my mouth with it,
and said, Lo, this hath touched thy lips.

and thine iniquity is taken away, and thy sin, forgiven.

The maiden from Nazareth, reflecting upon God's love for her, calls out,
My soul doth magnify the Lord,
My spirit exults in the God who is my Savior.
He has regarded the humiliation of this slave,
And, from this hour, all ages will count me blessed.

The congregation of Israel recognized that Moses had experienced God's love.
No longer did he resort to force, as he had before fleeing into the desert.
When Aaron and the people made the molten image,
Moses turned to God and said,
Oh, this people have sinned a great sin,
and have made them gods of gold,
Yet now, if thou wilt, forgive them...and if not -
Blot me out I pray thee, out of thy book which thou hast written.

They returned that love: they went after him in the wilderness,
they followed him in a land that was not sown.

What implications does this have for a congregation that accepts a person
who has experienced the love of God?

There is sensitivity to one another; there is listening; there is
forgiveness; there is freedom; there is joy, singing, caring.

The congregation gives freedom to the pastor to choose her or his friends,
which then can become an intimate support group.
The pastor listens attentively to the parishioners,
knowing that God speaks through them as well.

The congregation extends encouragement, becomes a family to the pastor,
lifts when the load of leadership becomes heavy,
prays for the pastor at evening prayers,
allows the pastor to be transparent, to be weak and helpless too.
The work load is shared with one another.
The congregation is aware that times of replenishment, getting away from
it all, recreation, are needed.

The pastor encourages the individuals, especially the young,
to find their God-given gifts and to develop them under God.
The leader touches the children with tenderness and loving kindness.
The leader walks more slowly with those who already see the distant horizon,
beyond, anticipating the realities of eternal life.
The leader empathizes with those in middle life--
who are pressed with so many responsibilities,
who in the rush of life sometimes forget to keep first things, first,
admonishing them to stay close to the Word of God.

Above all, the worshipping community holds out to one another the love of
Christ, so that those who look on confess with the first century onlookers,
See how they love one another.

The implications are many for a congregation which accepts a person
who has experienced the love of God.

Today is a special day.

Your pastor and his wife and you as a congregation are opening your hearts
to Martha Smith,
one who has responded to the call of God.

The impact of her call has been felt by her immediate family and friends,
by her larger circle of friends and associates,
by the congregations she has served in the past,
by the congregation she is and will be serving.

There is a quality in Martha's life that is difficult to define--
A humility, an "at peaceness," a sense of resignation, tranquility,
German says it best: "gelassenheit," "stille zu Gott."

I recall the different occasions over the past years, when Martha shared
    quietly,
"I can't get over the way the Lord has been leading in my life.
God has been so near, so real; I just marvel.
Who am I to experience all this?"

There is an obedience that characterizes her life.
I recall the occasion of the commissioning of John Howard Yoder
to the teaching of God's Word.
Bro. J.C. Wenger spoke of the insignia used by the Moravian Brethren--
the ox, standing between the plow and the altar,
waiting, to go in either direction.

From this hour,
As this congregation and Martha move into the work
for which she is being commissioned,
keep in mind the responsibilities for both pastor and congregation.
Both are involved
in the holiness of God,
in God's need for men and women,
in the authority of God,
and in the love of God.

GERTRUDE ROTEN originally preached this for the commissioning service of
Martha Smith (Good) on January 22, 1978 at Stirling Avenue Mennonite
Church, Kitchener, Ontario. She later adapted this for the commissioning
service of Sue Schantz, another former AMBS student. Gertrude teaches
Greek at the Seminary, as well as other New Testament courses. The scrip-
tural material she so authentically weaves in here comes from the American
Revised Standard version, her favorite.

WEAVING WISDOM
Sermons by
Mennonite Women

Why a collection of sermons? Several reasons are ready. Herein is diversity, truth, flavor, and proof.

Herein is diversity. Writers bring personal experience to their task. That includes being pastor, grandmother, seminary student, teacher, and activist. Diversity surfaces through city sensitivity and rural reflection, through language patterns and use of the Bible. Themes of Spirituality, Justice, and Story shape content.

Herein is truth. "Who is wise and understanding among you?" Thirty writers risk revealing their works, being both vulnerable and confident. They weave threads. The weave reflection. They weave into, around, and through rich strands of life and pain, fears and hope. They weave scriptural insight.

Herein is flavor. Hymns prove resourceful. The untried and the tested blend together. Humor emerges briefly, making one wish for more. The reader who looks for: "This I believe..." or "God is..." will know reward.

Herein is proof. Mennonite women are preaching and teaching. Not to be denied, this fact combines call and consent. The task demands while the content reenergizes. This window into our present decade reveals cooperative effort within congregations and communities. So be it.

Editor, Dorothy Yoder Nyce